The Chamber

JOHN GRISHAM

Level 6

Retold by Sue Harmes
Series Editors: Andy Hopkins and Jocelyn Potter

Pearson Education Limited
Edinburgh Gate, Harlow,
Essex CM20 2JE, England
and Associated Companies throughout the world.

ISBN 0 582 36411 6

First published in Great Britain by Century, one of the Publishers in
Random House UK Ltd 1994
This edition first published 1999
Second impression 2000

Original copyright © John Grisham 1994
Text copyright © Penguin Books 1999
All rights reserved

Typeset by Digital Type, London
Set in 11/14pt Bembo
Printed in Spain by Mateu Cromo, S. A. Pinto (Madrid)

Published by Pearson Education Limited in association with
Penguin Books Ltd, both companies being subsidiaries of Pearson Plc

For a complete list of the titles available in the Penguin Readers series please write to your local
Pearson Education office or to: Marketing Department, Penguin Longman Publishing,
5 Bentinck Street, London W1M 5RN.

Contents

Introduction

The horror of death row is that you die a little each day. The waiting kills you. You live in a cage – and when you wake up, you mark off another day and you tell yourself that you are now one day closer to death.

Seventy-year-old Sam Cayhall is on Mississippi's death row for a horrible crime he committed many years ago. Sam hates lawyers and wants to handle the final stages of the legal process himself. His date with the gas chamber is suddenly frighteningly close, and time seems to be running out for him. Then a young lawyer, Adam Hall, arrives and tries to persuade Sam that he needs his help. Adam brings with him a secret which may make the old man change his mind.

John Grisham was born in Arkansas, USA, in 1955 and grew up in a family of five children. He studied accounting and law in Mississippi, graduating in 1981.

Grisham became a lawyer, but was also involved in politics; in 1983 he was elected to the Mississippi House of Representatives. In 1984 he began to write his first book, *A Time to Kill*. His second book, *The Firm*, became a best-seller and made him famous. Grisham was then able to give up law to become a writer. All his books have now been best-sellers and six of them have been made into movies – *The Client*, *The Pelican Brief*, *The Firm*, *A Time to Kill*, *The Chamber*, and *The Rainmaker*.

Grisham lives in Virginia and Mississippi with his wife and two children. He has sold over 55 million copies of his books worldwide, and is one of the world's most popular writers.

Chapter 1   A Delicate Exercise

It began with a phone call on the night of April 17, 1967. Not trusting his own telephone, Jeremiah Dogan drove to a pay phone at a gas station to make the call. At the other end, Sam Cayhall listened to the instructions he was given. When he returned to bed, he told his wife nothing. She didn't ask.

Two days later, Cayhall left his home town of Clanton at dusk and drove to Greenville, Mississippi. There he drove slowly through the center of the city, and found the offices of the Jewish lawyer Marvin B. Kramer. It had been easy for the Klan★ to pick Kramer as their next target. He had a long history of support for the civil rights movement. He led protests against whites-only facilities. He accused public officials of racism. He had paid for the rebuilding of a black church destroyed by the Klan. He even welcomed Negroes to his home.

The operation had been simple to plan, as it involved only three people. Mississippi Klan leader Dogan provided the money, and enjoyed his role as organizer. The second man was Sam Cayhall, one of two men chosen by Dogan to do the actual dirty work. The Cayhall family's connections with the Klan went back very many years, but there was little Klan activity in Clanton so he was considered harmless by the FBI.† He was a good choice.

At eleven, Cayhall drove to Cleveland, where he looked for a green Pontiac. He found the vehicle parked at a truck stop on

---

★ The Ku Klux Klan: a secret terrorist organization (of 'Klansmen'), which began in the south of the USA, targeting blacks, Jews, and other groups.
† The FBI (Federal Bureau of Investigation): the government agency in the USA which investigates crimes relating to the country's security.

Highway 61, got in, and drove it out into open farming country. There he stopped on a lonely road and opened the trunk. In a box covered with newspapers, he found everything he needed. Then he drove back into town and waited at an all-night café.

At exactly 2 a.m., the third person in the team walked into the café and sat across from Sam Cayhall. This young man's name was Rollie Wedge. At the age of twenty-two, Rollie was already deeply committed to the struggle for white power. His father was in the construction industry, and had taught his son how to use explosives. Cayhall knew little about the young man, but they had done this kind of job together several times now and Rollie certainly knew what he was doing. They drank coffee together for half an hour. Sam's cup shook in his hand, but Rollie's was steady.

The two men climbed into the green Pontiac and, with Cayhall at the wheel, the car headed south on Highway 61. It was around 4 a.m. when they drove up to Kramer's office in Greenville. The street was very quiet and dark.

"This'll be easy," Rollie said softly. "Too bad we can't bomb his house, though."

"Yeah. Too bad," Sam agreed nervously. "But there's a guard at the house. And he's got kids in there, you know."

"Kill them while they're young," Rollie said. "Little Jews grow up to be big ones."

Cayhall parked the car in an alley behind Kramer's office. The men quietly opened the trunk, removed the box and Rollie's bag, and moved silently along to the door at the back of the office. Cayhall broke open the door and in seconds they were inside. In the main hallway was a closet filled with old legal files. The perfect place for the bomb.

"Stay by the door and watch the alley," Wedge whispered, and Sam did exactly as he was told. He preferred not to handle the explosives himself.

Rollie quickly set the box on the floor in the closet, and wired the dynamite. It was a delicate exercise, and Sam's heart raced as he waited. He kept his back to the explosives, just in case something went wrong. They were in the office less than five minutes.

In each of the bombings they had carried out before, Wedge had used a fifteen-minute fuse, lit with a match. The two bombers enjoyed being on the road, on the edge of the town, just as the bomb destroyed its target. With the car windows down, they had heard and felt each of the explosions at a comfortable distance.

But tonight was different. Sam made a wrong turn, and suddenly they were stopped at a railroad crossing as a long, slow train went through. Sam checked his watch. The train passed, and Sam took another wrong turn. The ground would shake in less than five minutes. Greenville was not a big city, and Sam guessed he must soon meet a familiar street. As he turned again, he realized he was going the wrong way down a one-way street. He hit the brakes hard, and the car stopped. He tried the engine, but it wouldn't start. Sam was shaking with fear.

"Stay calm," Rollie said slowly.

The minutes were passing. They could not be very far from the lawyer's office. When the bomb goes off, thought Sam, we might be too close for comfort.

He turned the key once more, and the car started this time. They sped away. More than fifteen minutes had passed since they had left the office. No explosion. At last Sam found himself in a street he knew, and began to head toward the edge of town.

"What kind of fuse did you use?" Sam finally asked, as they turned on to Highway 82. Rollie didn't reply. That was his business.

They slowed while they passed a parked police car, and then

gained speed out of town. Within minutes, Greenville was behind them, still quiet and at peace.

"What kind of fuse did you use?" Sam asked again, more loudly this time.

Rollie did not look at him. "I tried something new," he answered.

"What?"

"You wouldn't understand," Rollie said. Sam considered the possibilities.

"A timer?" he asked, a few miles down the road.

"Something like that."

◆

The horror of the Kramer bombing actually began about the time when Sam Cayhall was leaving Rollie Wedge back at the truck-stop café in Cleveland. Ruth Kramer's alarm clock went off around five-thirty in the morning, and she realized immediately that she was very sick. Her husband Marvin helped her to the bathroom and said he would take the five-year-old twins, Josh and John, to their nursery school. As soon as the boys were bathed, dressed, and fed, he said goodbye to Ruth, and he and the twins left the house. They were early, and as Marvin had some work to do before going into court for the morning, he decided to take the twins into the office with him before delivering them to nursery school.

The boys loved their father's office. When they arrived there around seven-thirty, they went straight to the secretary's desk, with its tempting pile of typing paper, scissors, and pens. Marvin looked in and began to lecture the twins about the mess, but they were running off down the hallway, not listening. Marvin smiled to himself.

At that time, none of the other staff had arrived at the office. Marvin's secretary, Helen, was on her way, just leaving the post office. His colleague, David Lukland, had just locked his apartment door three blocks away.

Marvin decided to go up to the third floor to find an old file which might help him with the case he was preparing. As he climbed the stairs, he could hear the little boys laughing somewhere down the hall. At about a quarter to eight, the huge explosion shot upward and horizontally at several thousand feet per second. The fifteen sticks of dynamite in the center of the wooden building destroyed it in seconds. It took a full minute for the pieces of wood, metal, and glass to return to earth.

Josh and John Kramer were less than fifteen feet from the bomb and were killed immediately. Their twisted little bodies were found under the ruins by local firemen. Marvin Kramer was thrown against the ceiling of the third floor, then fell through the great hole in the center of the building. He was found twenty minutes later and rushed to hospital. He lost both his legs.

A number of pedestrians in the street outside were also hurt. One of these injuries was minor but very significant. A stranger called Sam Cayhall was walking toward the Kramer office when the ground shook so hard he fell over. He was hit by flying glass. His face turned pale with horror at the sight before him, then he ran away. In shock, and with blood still running from him, he climbed into a green Pontiac and drove off. Two police officers were speeding toward the scene of the bombing. When they met the Pontiac, it stopped still, frozen in its traffic lane, refusing to move and let the police car through. The officers ran to the car, pulled open the door, and found a man covered in blood. They secured his wrists and forced him into the back of the police car. The Pontiac was taken away.

At the jail, they almost decided to release Sam on the minor charge of blocking the road to emergency vehicles. But then Detective Ivy saw him, bloody and pale-faced, and decided to ask him a few questions. He took Sam into his office. How did Sam's face get cut? He said that maybe he'd been in a fight. Where was the fight? Who was he fighting with? Where did it happen? Where did he get the car? Sam had no answers. His hands were shaking.

"Two little boys got blown to bits in their daddy's office this morning. A local lawyer by the name of Kramer . . . Jewish. Let me guess – you know nothing about it, right?" asked the detective.

"No. I'd like to see a lawyer," Sam said finally.

The piece of glass in Sam's face was removed and sent to the laboratory. It matched the glass in the front windows of the office building. The green Pontiac car was traced to Jeremiah Dogan. A fifteen-minute fuse was found in its trunk. Sam Cayhall was also found to be a longtime member of the Klan. The case was solved as far as the FBI was concerned. Rollie Wedge's name was not mentioned, and would not be spoken by either Dogan or Cayhall. They feared for their own homes and families if they did.

◆

Sam Cayhall and Jeremiah Dogan were charged with murder on May 5, 1967. Their lawyer, Clovis Brazelton, made sure that the trial was held many miles away, in Nettles County, an area sympathetic to the Klan.

"You don't think I'll be found guilty?" Sam asked him.

"Of course not. You just deny everything." Brazelton patted Sam on the arm. "Trust me, Sam, I've done this before. We'll get an all-white jury. Your kind of people."

Outside the courthouse, the Klan set up camp. Supporters arrived from other states, and their leaders made long speeches calling Cayhall and Dogan their heroes.

Inside the courtroom, things went smoothly for the two men. Brazelton raised doubts about the prosecution's case. Most importantly, no one actually saw Cayhall putting the bomb in the office. In fact, no one could prove anything.

After a day and a half of hard discussion, the jury could not agree whether the men were guilty or not. The trial was abandoned, and Sam Cayhall went home for the first time in five months.

◆

The second trial was held six months later, in another rural area four hours from Greenville. This area too was full of Klan members and people sympathetic to them. The jury again was all-white and non-Jewish. They heard the same stories, the same lies.

This trial did have something new. Marvin Kramer was there, sitting in his wheelchair next to the front row. He watched the jury for three days. Most of them could not bear to look at him. However, one young woman glanced at Marvin repeatedly – Sharon Culpepper was the mother of twin boys. As Marvin looked back at her, his eyes begged her for justice.

When the jury went away to discuss the case, Sharon Culpepper alone voted the men guilty. For two days the rest of the jury tried to make her change her mind, but she was firm. The second trial ended with the jury undecided, eleven to one. Again, everyone was sent home.

Rollie Wedge's name had been mentioned only once. During a lunch break, Dogan whispered to Cayhall that a message had been received from the kid. Wedge wanted them to know that he was in the area, watching the trial, and watching them.

◆

Ruth and Marvin Kramer separated in 1970. He entered a mental hospital later that year, and in 1971 he killed himself. He was buried next to his sons.

Ruth Kramer returned to Memphis to live with her parents.

7

They wanted Cayhall and Dogan to go on trial for a third time. In fact, the whole Jewish community in Greenville was angry when it became apparent that the District Attorney was tired of losing. There was no new evidence, and a prosecution looked hopeless. Despite pressure from the FBI, the possibility of a new trial gradually faded.

By the late 1970s, many things had changed. Civil rights had arrived in Mississippi. Blacks were voting. Black children went to school with white children. The Klan had not succeeded in keeping Negroes where they belonged.

Then in 1979, two events occurred in the inactive Kramer bombing case. The first was the election of David McAllister as the District Attorney in Greenville. At twenty-seven he was the youngest DA in the state's history. As a teenager, he had stood with the crowd in front of the ruins of Marvin Kramer's office. Now he promised to bring the terrorists to justice.

The second event was an investigation by the tax authorities of Jeremiah Dogan's financial affairs. They produced eighty-six charges against him, relating to non-payment of taxes, which could lead to a maximum of twenty-eight years in prison. After much discussion, the government offered Dogan a deal. They would not jail him for the tax avoidance if he gave evidence against Sam Cayhall in a new trial of the Kramer case. Dogan accepted the offer.

◆

After twelve years of living quietly in Ford County, Sam Cayhall found himself once again on trial. Much had changed. All-white juries were now rare. There were black judges and black lawyers.

The trial began in February 1981, in a little courthouse in Lakehead County. The young and ambitious District Attorney, David McAllister, did a fine job for the prosecution. He looked good and spoke with feeling to the jury of eight whites and four blacks. He told them how, as a child in Greenville, he had grown up with Jewish friends and had played with black kids too. He told them how, one morning in 1967, he had seen the smoking ruins of Kramer's office. He saw the firemen finding Marvin Kramer, then the bodies of the boys. Tears had run down his cheeks as they slowly carried the little bodies to an ambulance. When McAllister's speech finished, the courtroom was silent. Several members of the jury had tears in their eyes.

On February 12, 1981, Sam Cayhall was found guilty of murder. Two days later, the jury decided he should be put to death. He was taken to Parchman prison to begin his long wait for the gas chamber. He was now on death row.

Chapter 2   Kravitz and Bane

With 286 lawyers, Kravitz and Bane was the third largest law firm in Chicago. Appropriately, its fashionable offices filled the top floors of the third largest building downtown. The firm earned most of its huge income from commercial and insurance cases. Like most large firms, it made so much money that it felt it had an obligation to society to take a few worthwhile cases without charge. There was a full-time partner dealing with these cases, an eccentric do-gooder named E. Garner Goodman. He worked for clients who could not afford to pay: death row prisoners, people on drugs, and the homeless.

Adam Hall headed along the hallway, toward Goodman's office. Hall was twenty-six years old, and had been employed by Kravitz and Bane for nine months now. He held a thin file in his hand, a summary of his education and career.

In Goodman's disorganized office, Adam sat and waited

nervously while the gray-haired old man studied the file.

"This is a pretty strong recommendation." He was reading a letter from Wycoff, the partner responsible for Adam. "You're bright. You work very hard. The firm is lucky to have you. And you want to work with me? Why? Let me guess. You want to help other people, do some honest work, give something back to your community?"

"Not really," admitted Adam.

"So what is it you have in mind, then?"

Adam cleared his throat. "It's a death penalty case."

"A death penalty case?" Goodman repeated. "Why?"

"Well, I'm opposed to the death penalty."

"Aren't we all?" Goodman closed the file. "Look, Mr. Hall, these are high pressure cases. Life and death. You're too young and you don't have the experience to handle something like this."

"I want to take on the Cayhall case," Adam said slowly.

Goodman shook his head. "Sam Cayhall just fired us. And frankly, I'm relieved to have him out of my life."

"The man needs a lawyer."

"No he doesn't. He'll be dead in three months with or without one. He's decided to represent himself."

"He needs a lawyer," Adam repeated. "I think so, and I've studied his entire file."

Goodman thought about this. "That's a lot of paper. Why did you do it?"

"It's an interesting case."

"Sam Cayhall is not a nice man. He's a racist who hates just about everybody. He hates lawyers. He'd hate you."

"I don't think so. I want the chance to meet him."

Goodman folded his hands in front of him. "Why, may I ask, are you so determined to work on this particular case?"

Adam paused. "I have a secret for you, Mr. Goodman. You

must promise not to reveal it to anyone, OK?"

"You have my promise."

Adam took a deep breath. "I'm related to Sam Cayhall."

Goodman stared at him. Adam explained, "Sam Cayhall had a son, Eddie. Eddie Cayhall left Mississippi when his father was arrested for the bombing. He ran to California with his young family, changed his name, and tried to forget. But he suffered terribly. He killed himself soon after his father was found guilty in 1981. Eddie Cayhall was my father."

"Sam Cayhall is your grandfather?"

"Yes. I didn't know it until I was almost seventeen."

"That was when your father killed himself?"

"Right. I'll spare you the details, but I found his body, and I cleaned up the mess before my mother and sister returned home. After we buried my father, my Aunt Lee told me the truth about Sam Cayhall. Since then I've read everything I can about the case."

"And you think Sam will trust you as his lawyer?"

"I don't know. All I know is he's my grandfather and I have to go and see him."

"You should've told someone about this when you joined the firm."

"I know. But nobody asked if my grandfather was a client of the firm."

Goodman made a decision. "We'll work something out. I'll need to present this to the other partners. They won't like it, but I'll make them agree. You'll have to persuade your grandfather. You'll be the front man and we'll give you all the help we can." He paused. "Then, when they kill him, we'll be around to support you."

"It's not hopeless, is it?"

"Almost. We've handled Sam's appeals for seven years now, and they've all failed. A new execution date will be chosen any day now. Probably late summer. I have to warn you – it will be very nasty, Mr. Hall. I've watched three of my clients die. If they kill him, you'll never be the same again."

◆

It was after midnight. Adam sat on the sofa in his tiny apartment. The room was dark, except for the light from the television screen. The video he was watching was one he had pieced together over the years. *The Adventures of a Klan Bomber*, he called it. It started with a television news report from 1967 about the bombing of a Jewish church.

The Kramer bombing was next. People were seen running to the remains of Marvin's office, while the police tried to push them back. A cloud of dust and smoke hung over the ruins. Voices shouted and the camera rocked as it captured the shocking scene.

The video cut from the bombing scene to the front of the jail, where Sam Cayhall was being led to a car. It was 1967, twenty-three years ago. Sam was forty-six years old. At that time Adam was a little boy, known as Alan Cayhall; soon after that he was taken to a distant state where he was given a new name. Now Adam pressed the pause button and stared for the millionth time into the face of his grandfather.

The video continued with more pictures of Sam outside various jails and courthouses. One scene showed Marvin Kramer after the second trial. He was in his wheelchair on the sidewalk outside the courthouse. He suddenly saw two Klansmen dressed in white and began shouting at them. They made some cruel remark, and Marvin went crazy, screaming and cursing. He spun the metal wheels of his chair, chasing after them, the cameras recording it all. The wheelchair turned over, and Marvin fell out on to the grass, crying in an odd high-pitched voice.

When the video ended, Adam stared at the blank screen. Behind the sofa were three large boxes which contained the rest of the story: endless pages of notes on all three trials; copies of all the documents relating to the case since the last trial; hundreds of newspaper stories about Sam; notes from law school. Adam knew more about his grandfather than anyone alive. But he also knew that the man was still a mystery to him.

♦

Adam and his sister Carmen first met their Aunt Lee at their father's funeral. Her name had been mentioned occasionally, but as children they were taught not to ask questions about family. All they knew was that she lived in Memphis, had married into a rich Memphis family, and had no contact with her brother Eddie because of some ancient family fight. After her brother's funeral, Lee stayed for two weeks and spent time with her nephew and niece. They loved her because she was pretty and cool; she took them shopping, and to the movies, and for long walks by the ocean.

And it was Aunt Lee who sat with Adam and at last told him something about his family. She told him about Sam's Klan activities, and the Kramer bombing, and the trials that eventually sent him to death row in Mississippi. Adam's interest was awakened. It was an awful story, but at least there was a family out there! Perhaps he wasn't so unusual after all. Perhaps there were aunts and uncles and cousins with lives to share and stories to tell. But Lee was wise and quick enough to recognize this interest. She explained that the Cayhalls were not friendly and warm people, but a strange and secretive family who kept themselves apart.

Lee told Adam something of her childhood, living on a small farm fifteen minutes from Clanton. Sam was a decent father but not affectionate. Her mother was a weak woman who died of cancer. About her adult life Lee told Adam very little. She had left home at the age of eighteen and married Phelps Booth, who came from a rich banking family. They seemed to have had a miserable marriage.

Lee stayed with Adam's family for two weeks after the funeral, then left. They had occasionally exchanged letters and cards, but had seen little of each other since then.

Their conversation on the phone last night had been brief. When Adam said he would be living in Memphis for a few months, and would like to see her, Lee invited him to her luxury apartment by the river. He would live with her, she insisted. She was now living apart from her husband, and he would be company. Then he said he would be working in the Memphis office, working on Sam's case, in fact.

♦

Adam pushed Lee's doorbell at a few minutes after nine. Lee opened the door and they kissed.

"Welcome," she said.

She led him out onto the patio overlooking the river.

"It's good to see you," she said with a nice smile. She was almost fifty, and had aged a lot. Her hair was now going gray, and her soft blue eyes were red and worried.

They talked about Adam's sister Carmen, studying psychology at Berkeley, and about his mother, who had got married again to a man who made a fortune in timber. But Adam was in no mood for small talk.

"I'm going to see Sam tomorrow."

Lee poured them both a large whisky. "Why?"

"Why not? Because he's my grandfather. Because he's going to die. Because I'm a lawyer and he needs help."

"He doesn't even know you."

"He will tomorrow. I'll tell him who I am. I'm sick of Cayhall secrets. When I was a kid, every time I asked questions about my family, Mother would tell me to stop because it might upset my father. I want to know about the family, Lee, however bad it really is."

"It's awful," she whispered, almost to herself.

"But do you care? Have you been to see Sam?"

"Don't start this, Adam. You don't understand."

"Explain it to me then. I want to understand."

"It's not easy to talk about. Just give me some time."

"I may be in Memphis for months."

"I want you to stay here. We'll need each other." She hesitated. "I mean, he is going to die, isn't he?"

"It's likely."

"Then why are you getting involved?"

"I don't know. Maybe it's because I don't believe that he intended to kill those kids. There's something that doesn't add up." He paused. "How many people know you're Sam's daughter? Do your husband's family know?"

"Very few people know. I'd like to keep it that way."

"You're ashamed of —"

"Yes, I'm ashamed of my father! Who wouldn't be?" Her words were suddenly sharp and bitter. "He's killed enough people — the Kramer twins, their father, your father, and God knows who else."

"You feel no pity for him?"

"Occasionally. I think about him all the time. I've wondered a million times how my father became such a horrible person. Why did my father have to be a Klansman who killed innocent children and ruined his own family?"

Adam saw that tears were running down her face.

"I'm sorry," he said, "I'm so sorry, Lee."

Chapter 3   Parchman

After twenty-three years, Adam was finally returning to the state of his birth. He drove across the flat plain of the Mississippi, following the traffic south. He was on Highway 61, which for decades had served as the principal route for hundreds of thousands of poor blacks journeying north to Memphis and Chicago and Detroit in search of jobs and decent housing. The fields of beans and cotton grew vast and ran to the horizon. Though it was not yet nine o'clock, the weather was already hot and sticky.

At Clarksdale, he left Highway 61 and headed southeast on 49. Eventually a road sign declared that Parchman prison was ahead. Soon, he saw the buildings. There were no tall chain-link fences to prevent escape. Instead, Adam saw an entrance and several buildings facing the highway. As he approached, a woman in uniform stepped from a guardhouse. He lowered his window.

"I'm a lawyer, here to see a client on death row," Adam said weakly, aware of how nervous he sounded.

"We've got nobody on death row, sir."

"I'm sorry?"

"No such place as death row. We've got lots of them in the Maximum Security Unit, that's MSU for short, but you won't find no death row here."

"OK."

"Name?" she said.

"Adam Hall."

"And your client?"

"Sam Cayhall." She seemed unimpressed, and after a few more questions sent him on his way. Small buildings and trees on each side of the main prison road made this more like a pleasant street in a small town than a prison with 5,000 inmates. An arrow on a road sign pointed left to the Maximum Security Unit. A dirt road led quickly to some 12-foot high fencing. The unit was a single-story flat roof building of red brick.

Adam stepped unsteadily from his car and stared at the building. He looked up to the watchtower. A gate slid open a few feet so he could enter, then closed behind him. A second gate opened. As Adam went through, a huge guard with a thick neck and arms as big as Adam's legs approached.

He held out an enormous black hand and said, "Sergeant Packer." Adam shook the hand. "Adam Hall."

"Here to see Sam."

"Yes, sir."

"Your first visit?" They walked toward the building.

"Yeah. Are all death row inmates here?"

"Yes, all forty-seven." They were at the door. "I have to search you."

He took Adam's briefcase from him, and put it down on the ground. Then he ran his hands up his legs, around his body, and under his arms, patting expertly around in search of hidden weapons. The search was over in seconds. "Not a good day to see Sam," he said.

"Why's that?" Adam asked, following Packer.

"Didn't you know? They've fixed a new date for the execution. The big day is four weeks away. August 8."

"Four weeks!" Adam said, shocked.

"Afraid so. Papers came from the Mississippi Supreme Court this morning."

Adam entered the conference room. Four weeks.

◆

The room was empty. It was a large room divided by a solid wall of brick and metal; the lawyers had their side and the clients had theirs. The lower wall was made of brick, then there was a

17

counter for the lawyers' papers. A green metal screen ran from there up to the ceiling.

"I have to lock this door," Packer said as he stepped outside. "We'll get Sam." The door closed, and Adam was alone. His stomach was turning over violently.

Adam began chewing his fingernails. In the center of the screen in front of him was a gap, four inches by ten, and it was through this little hole that he would come face-to-face with Sam Cayhall.

Adam jumped as a door was unlocked. The door opened slowly, and a young white guard stepped into the inmates' side. Behind him, in a bright red cotton jumpsuit, was Sam Cayhall. He frowned, looking hard at the screen, until his eyes landed on Adam. "Who are you?" he spat. The guard led him across to a spot directly across from the lawyer and sat him in a chair. Sam stared at Adam as the guard departed.

This was it, the Cayhall version of a family reunion.

"I'm Adam Hall. I'm a lawyer with Kravitz and Bane."

Sam took his card and examined it. Adam watched him. Sam was an old man now, with pale delicate skin and tiny lines around his eyes. His hair was long, gray, and oily. Deep lines of age and sadness cut into his forehead. The only attractive feature was the set of deep blue eyes that now looked up at Adam. "You Jew boys never give up, do you?" he asked.

"I'm not Jewish," Adam said, returning the stare.

"Then how can you work for Kravitz and Bane?" His words were soft, slow, and delivered with the patience of a man who'd spent nine and a half years alone in a tiny cell.

"We're an equal opportunity employer."

"Oh, sure. How many women partners do you have? How many blacks?" Sam lit a cigarette. "I thought I was finished with you people."

"They didn't send me down here. I volunteered."

"Why are you so nervous?"

Adam pulled his fingernails away from his teeth. "I'm not nervous."

"Sure you are. I've seen lots of lawyers around here, and I've never seen one as nervous as you. What's the matter, kid? You afraid I'm coming through the screen after you?"

"Don't be silly." Adam tried to smile.

"How old are you?"

"Twenty-six."

"You look twenty-two. You just finished law school?"

"Last year."

"You've handled death cases before? How many?"

"This is the first."

"Just great. Those Jewish-American lawyers at Kravitz and Bane sent you down here to experiment on me, right? I've known for a long time that they secretly wanted me dead, now this proves it."

"You need a lawyer, Mr. Cayhall. I'm here to help."

"I need a lot of things, boy, but I sure as hell don't need a beginner like you. Do you realize, son, that I get at least three offers a week now from lawyers who want to represent me for nothing? Big lawyers. Well-known lawyers. You see, son, I'm famous. There'll be a book deal, a movie deal, a television series. I'm worth a lot of money."

Adam was shaking his head. "I don't want any of that. I'll sign a confidentiality agreement."

"The fact is, Mr. Hall, I hate lawyers." He leaned forward slightly and stared at Adam through the hole in the screen. "You're twenty-six, you say?"

"Yeah."

"Born in 1964."

"That's right."

Sam gave this some thought. "Where?"

"Memphis," Adam replied, without looking at him.

"What you've got to understand, son, is that this state needs an execution, and I'm the nearest victim. Louisiana, Texas, and Florida are killing them like flies, and the people of this state can't understand why our little chamber is not being used. The more violent crime we have, the more people beg for executions. It's my turn, and you can't stop it. So where did you grow up?"

"Southern California. LA."

"Did you know the law has just been changed here? Now we can die by injection. It's less cruel. Isn't that nice? It doesn't apply to me though, since my conviction was years ago. I'll smell the gas. Are your family still in California?"

For a second, Adam's heart stopped beating. He sank a few inches in his chair. "My father's dead."

A long minute passed. Sam said, "And your mother?"

"She lives in Portland. Remarried."

"Where's your sister?" he asked.

Adam closed his eyes and dropped his head. "She's in college."

Sam's next words were softly spoken. "I believe her name's Carmen, right?"

Adam nodded. "How did you know?" he asked.

"The voice. You sound like your father. Why'd you come here?"

"Eddie sent me."

Their eyes met briefly, then Sam looked away. He placed his right hand over his eyes.

"We need to talk," Adam said quietly.

Sam nodded. "So you're really Alan," he said. "My first grandson. You disappeared in 1967."

"Something like that. I don't remember that far back."

"I heard Eddie went to California, and that there was another child. Someone told me later her name was Carmen." He closed

20

his eyes tightly for a moment. "When did you find out about me?"

"Not until after my father's funeral. Lee told me."

Sam relaxed a bit in his chair. "Listen to me, kid. I can see you've been planning this for a long time. But you can't be my lawyer. First, I'm beyond help. They're determined to gas me, for lots of reasons. Second, your true identity will be revealed. It'll be very embarrassing."

"Look, I don't care if the world knows that I'm your grandson. I'm tired of all these dirty little family secrets."

"You don't understand, kid."

"So explain it to me. We have four weeks. You can do a lot of talking in four weeks."

"Exactly what is it that you want to hear?"

Adam leaned closer to the screen. "First, I want to talk about the case – appeals, how we handle the legal process, the bombing, who was with you that night –"

"No one was with me that night."

"We'll talk about that. Second, I want to know about my family. I want to know about your father and his father, and your brother and cousins. I have the right to know about them. And I want to know about Eddie."

Sam took a deep breath and closed his eyes. "You don't want much, do you?" he said softly.

Adam reached into his briefcase and removed a thin file. He slid a sheet of paper and a pen through the opening.

"This is an agreement for legal representation. Sign at the bottom."

Sam took the paper. He read it slowly. "I'll need some time to think about this, Adam. Let me look over this, make some changes, and we'll meet again tomorrow."

"That's wasting time."

"I've wasted ten years here. What's another day?"

Adam put his pen in his pocket and picked up his briefcase. "I'll be working out of our Memphis office. The number's on the card. Feel free to call anytime."

Sam slowly stood up. "Just make sure you come back."

"I promise."

♦

The Memphis offices of Kravitz and Bane were large, thickly carpeted, and richly decorated. Adam was met by an attractive young secretary and taken to the corner office of Baker Cooley, the managing partner.

"Welcome south," Cooley said.

"Thanks. I guess you've talked to Garner Goodman."

"Twice. He told me what you'll be doing. We've got a nice room at the end of this hall with a phone, computer, lots of space. It's yours for, uh, however long you need it."

Adam nodded. "What kind of work goes on here?"

"Mostly company stuff. We represent some old banks, and we do a lot of local government work. Certainly no criminal work," he added quickly, as if criminals were not welcome in his respectable offices.

"I hope I won't be in the way here."

"Not at all. I'm afraid we won't be much help, though. We're not trial lawyers."

"I'll be fine. Mr. Goodman and the guys there will help."

Cooley rubbed his hands as if he wasn't sure what else to do with them. "There is one thing, though. Got a call a couple of hours ago from a reporter here in Memphis. Asking about the Cayhall case. I suggested he contact the boys in Chicago." He crossed his arms on his chest. "Look, Adam, we like to avoid publicity here."

"You don't want any of the dirt to rub off on you?"

"Not at all, no. It's just that things are different here. We don't deal with criminals. We have to be concerned about our reputation. You know what I mean?"

"No."

"Look, Adam, this is a Chicago case, handled by you guys up there. Memphis has nothing to do with it, OK?"

"This office is part of Kravitz and Bane."

"Yeah, and this office has nothing to gain by being connected to dirt like Sam Cayhall."

Adam looked at him steadily. "Sam Cayhall is my grandfather."

Chapter 4   On Death Row

The news of Sam's new death sentence was whispered from cell to cell. On the Row, the death of one could mean the death of all. As Clyde Packer walked slowly along the hallway, he noticed that the inmates were quieter than usual. Several were looking through their court files.

Sergeant Packer had worked on the Row for twenty-one years. For eight hours each morning, he was in charge of fourteen prisoners and two guards. MSU was not a bad place to work. The inmates were generally quiet and well-behaved. They spent twenty-three hours a day alone in their cells. They were allowed an hour of outdoor exercise per day. Fourteen cells faced the hallway, each 6 feet wide and 9 feet deep. The front of each cell was a wall of iron bars, so that an inmate could never be completely private. Anything he did – sleep, use the toilet – could be observed by the guards.

Packer hated executions, but fortunately they had been rare in Mississippi. He'd been through only four since 1982. He came to number six cell, Sam's cell. It was less than ninety feet from the gas chamber.

Sam was sitting on the edge of his bed. "Mornin', Sam."

"Mornin', Packer," Sam replied. He was wearing a dirty white T-shirt and shorts, the usual dress for inmates in their cells because it was so hot. The bright red jumpsuits had to be worn when they went outside.

"Your lawyer said he was coming back today."

"Yeah. I guess I need lots of lawyers, huh, Packer?"

"Looks like it." He went on to check on his other boys.

The one light in the cell was above the stainless steel sink. Under the sink was a stainless steel toilet. Sam had few possessions: the most valuable was a collection of law books he had gathered over the years. They were placed neatly on shelves across from his bed. In a box on the floor was a large pile of files, Sam's legal history.

Sam went over to the calendar on the wall. Today was July 12. He had twenty-seven days.

He sat on the bed, picking up Adam's agreement. He had made neat, detailed notes along the edge of the page. Then he had added extra paragraphs on the back of the sheets. Another idea came to him, and he found room to add it. He took down his ancient typewriter, balanced it on his knees, put a sheet of paper in, and began typing.

♦

Retired Colonel George Nugent marched into the office of his boss Phillip Naifeh, superintendent at Parchman.

"Have a seat, George," Naifeh said to his assistant.

"Yes, sir." Nugent lowered himself carefully into the seat so that he would not spoil his perfectly ironed shirt and pants. His haircut was military, very short. Nugent was fifty-two and had served in Korea and Vietnam. He had been at Parchman as assistant superintendent for two years. He was dependable, and he

24

loved rules. It was no secret that the colonel wanted Naifeh's job in a couple of years.

"George, I've been looking at the Cayhall matter. I don't know how much you know about the appeals, but we could be looking at an execution in four weeks."

"Yes, sir, I read about it in today's paper."

"Did you miss the Parris execution?" asked Naifeh.

"Yes, sir. By a few weeks," he answered with a trace of disappointment.

"So you haven't been through one?"

"No, sir."

"Well, they're awful, George, just awful. Frankly, I don't think I can cope with this one. I need some help."

Nugent's back straightened even more. He nodded quickly, eyes dancing in all directions.

Naifeh continued. "So I was thinking that maybe you'd do a good job with this one."

The colonel couldn't stop himself smiling. Then the smile disappeared and he looked serious again.

"I'm sure I can handle it, sir."

"I'm sure you can too." Naifeh pointed to a black book on his desk. "We have a manual. There it is, the collected wisdom of two dozen visits to the gas chamber."

Nugent noticed that the pages of the book were a mess. The cover was worn and dirty. That would be his first job. The paperwork would be perfectly organized by the time he had finished with it.

"I'll read it tonight, sir." Nugent left the office, carrying the black book carefully, like a kid with a new toy.

He's crazy, thought Naifeh to himself, but he'll do a marvelous job of killing Sam Cayhall.

♦

Adam's two-page agreement was now four, neatly typed. He read it through slowly. He took a few notes and was amused at some of the language. But on the whole it was not bad for a non-lawyer.

"You do pretty good work," Adam said, as Sam smoked a cigarette and stared at him. "Though it's basically the same agreement I handed you yesterday."

"It's completely different," Sam said.

Adam glanced at his notes. "You seem to be concerned about five areas. The governor, books, movies, your right to end this agreement when you want, and the choice of witnesses to your execution."

"Those are the most important ones."

"I promised yesterday I would have nothing to do with books and movies. You can have complete confidentiality."

"Good."

"You want the right to end this agreement at any time."

"It took me a long time to get rid of Kravitz and Bane last time. I don't want to go through that again. And I want to deal with no one except you. That place is full of Jews, and they don't get involved, OK?"

"You will only be dealing with me," Adam assured him.

Adam read again a paragraph on page three. It gave Sam the authority to select two witnesses at his execution.

"I don't understand this," Adam said.

"It's very simple. If we get to that point, there will be about fifteen witnesses. I select two of them."

"Then why do you want this clause?"

"Because the lawyer is always one of the two."

"And you don't want me to witness the execution?"

"Correct." He leaned forward until his nose was an inch from the screen. "I do not want you there."

26

"It's a deal," said Adam easily. "We're not going to get that far, Sam."

"Good boy. That's what I want to hear."

Adam looked down at the agreement again. Almost an entire page was used on a violent attack on the state governor, David McAllister.

"So you have a problem with the governor," Adam said.

Sam's face was suddenly hard, his eyes narrow. "You listen to me, Adam. You are never to talk to that man. He's got a pretty smile and a clean haircut, but underneath it he's thoroughly dishonest. He is the reason I'm sitting here on death row. If you contact him in any way, you're finished as my lawyer."

"The governor could save your life, Sam."

"He put me here. Why would he want to do that?"

"I didn't say he wanted to. I said that he could."

Sam raised his eyes as if this kid was the stupidest human he'd met in decades. "If you think David McAllister will grant me a last-minute pardon, then you're a fool. But let me tell you what he will do. He'll use you, and me, to get all the publicity imaginable. He'll invite you to his office. Afterward, he'll hold a couple of interviews with the media and tell them everything you've just told him. The closer I get to the gas chamber, the more media attention there'll be."

"He can do this without us."

"And he will. An hour before I die, he'll hold a press conference. He'll stand there in front of a hundred cameras and explain why he can't pardon me. What a great story! We might even get him reelected."

"It won't hurt to talk to him."

"Fine. Talk to him. And after you do, I'll send you straight back to Chicago. Now, are you going to sign?"

"Yes."

"Then do it."

Adam signed at the bottom of the back page and handed it to Sam. Sam signed his name next to Adam's.

"Look, Adam. I need to know. What are my chances?"

"Depends on several things, Sam. Depends on how much you tell me about the bombing."

"I don't follow."

"If there are new facts, then we present them."

"What kind of new facts?"

Adam looked at him steadily. "Where did you learn to handle explosives?"

"Here and there."

"There were at least five bombings before Kramer, all the same type, all very basic — dynamite, a fuse lit with a match. Kramer of course was different because a timer was used. Who taught you how to make one?"

"It's very simple. Any fool could do it."

"Let's try it this way. Did you or did you not have someone with you, someone who placed the explosives, on the night when you bombed the Kramer office?"

Sam took his time in replying. The delay was significant.

"No," Sam said softly but firmly.

"I don't believe you, Sam. Why did you use a timer? Why did you want to delay the bomb?"

"I was tired of having to light the fuse and run like hell."

"What time was it supposed to go off?"

"Around five."

"What went wrong?"

"It didn't go off at five. It went off just before eight, and there were people in the building by then, and some of these people got killed. That's why I'm sitting here today."

"Where did you go when you left Kramer's office?"

"I found a little coffee shop on the highway. I had some coffee and cake and waited for the explosion. I always liked to hear the bombs go off and watch the people react."

"How long did you stay there?"

"A long time. I left a few minutes before six and drove past Kramer's office. The place looked fine. I went for a drive and returned to Greenville at seven. No explosion. I walked around. The thing wouldn't go off."

"Did you see Kramer and his sons go into the building?"

"No. I turned a corner and saw his car there. I thought about all the secretaries and other people who might work in there. I thought maybe I should make a phone call to the office, without giving my name, and warn them."

"Why didn't you?"

"I didn't have any change. I didn't want to walk into a store and ask for change. I was a stranger in the town. Everybody remembers strangers when there's a crime. I was really nervous. I kept thinking about all the people who worked in Kramer's office. It was almost eight o'clock and I knew the office opened in a few minutes. I knew a lot of people were going to get killed. My mind stopped working."

"Where did you go?"

"Toward the office. I saw a car park in front of the office next door. I think I was walking toward the car when the bomb went off."

"So you were across the street?"

"I think so. I remember being on my hands and knees as the glass fell all around me. But I don't remember much after that."

Adam looked at his watch and was suddenly tired. "I'd better go," he said. "I'll be back tomorrow."

"I'll be here."

"Lee's worried about you, Sam. She wanted me to tell you she's thinking about you."

Sam nodded slowly. Then he got up and knocked on the door behind him. He turned and looked at Adam until a guard opened the door and took him away.

Chapter 5   Identities

The Auburn House had never been a house or a home, but for decades it had been a little church of yellow brick and colored glass. It sat surrounded by an ugly chain-link fence a few blocks from downtown Memphis. A security guard walked along by the fence ready to open the gate. A block behind was the decaying housing project from which the patients of Auburn House came.

They were all teenage mothers, whose mothers had also been teenagers and whose fathers were generally unknown. The average age was fifteen. The youngest had been eleven. They walked to Auburn House because cars were scarce and they were too young to drive.

Adam parked at the side of the building and asked the guard for directions. Inside he saw half a dozen young girls sitting in plastic chairs with children at their feet. Lee was waiting for him along the hallway. They kissed each other.

"What exactly do you do here?" he asked her.

"We work with young mothers. Auburn House is a nonprofit organization staffed by volunteers," Lee replied. "Come into my office and I'll tell you about it."

They stepped inside and Adam looked at the colorful charts on the walls, giving advice on looking after babies.

"Sixty percent of the babies in this county are born to unmarried mothers," Lee explained. "Each year there are more cases of hurt and abandoned children. It'll break your heart. Some of these little fellows don't have a chance."

"How many hours a week do you work here?"

"I don't know. Who counts them? I get here around ten and leave after dark. I'm lucky. I can afford to work here full-time. Phelps has plenty of money."

"I admire you for this, Lee," Adam said slowly. "I often wondered what you did with your time."

"I had a job once. Phelps found me a job with one of his friends' companies. Big salary, nice office. I left after a year. I married money, Adam, so I'm not supposed to work. Phelps' mother was shocked that I wanted to work."

"What do rich women do all day?"

"The servants have to be directed and organized. There's always shopping to do. There are lunches, tea parties, dinners. It's a hard life."

"So why did you give up this hard life and move out?"

"I was not a very good rich woman, Adam. I hated it. It was fun for a very short time, but I didn't fit in. Also, Phelps' office is filled with beautiful women with short skirts and long legs who sit behind nice desks and talk on the phone and wait for him to call them. He has a small bedroom next to a conference room. The man's an animal."

"But you stay married to him?"

"I still make appearances. It's important for Phelps to have a wife who can show herself at social events. His family hate me, but they're the reason we stay married. A divorce would be unthinkable."

Adam laughed and shook his head. "This is crazy."

"Yes, but it works. I'm happy. He's happy."

"I saw Sam again today, Lee." Lee sank into her seat, and placed her feet on the desk. "I'm his lawyer."

"He signed the agreement?"

"Yes, he prepared one himself, four pages."

"What does Sam look like?"

"A very old man. Lots of lines on his face and pale skin. He's too old to be locked up in a cage."

Lee took his hand. "I'm sorry you're in the middle of all this," she whispered.

"I'm sorry too."

"Sorry about what?"

"I talked to a reporter with the *Memphis Press* earlier. They've heard the rumor that Sam Cayhall is my grandfather. I didn't tell him about you, but he'll find out."

"What do you think will happen?"

"My name will be in the paper tomorrow – Adam Hall, lawyer from Chicago, and grandson. And maybe you'll be named as the daughter of Sam Cayhall, murderer, racist, terrorist, the oldest man ever led to the gas chamber."

"I've been through worse."

"What?"

"Being the wife of Phelps Booth."

Adam laughed at this, and Lee managed a smile.

Then she grew serious and leaned forward. "Adam, there's something I need to tell you. I'm an alcoholic."

He was shocked. They'd had drinks together the last two nights.

"It's been about ten years now," she explained in a low voice. "There were lots of reasons, OK, some of which you can probably guess. I've been through treatment three times. It's not easy."

"How did it happen to you?"

"Gradually. I met Phelps, and he comes from a family of social drinkers. Then, when we started to have problems with our marriage, it was an escape."

"I hope I'm not the reason you started drinking again."

"No, but I need your help. You'll be living with me, and we'll have some bad times. Just help me."

"Sure, Lee. I'll help you."

◆

The horror of death row is that you die a little each day. The waiting kills you. You live in a cage – and when you wake up, you mark off another day and you tell yourself that you are now one day closer to death. At times, death would be welcome. But there is always hope, always the slight promise that in our strange system of justice, someone somewhere will decide to reverse his case. Every resident of the Row dreams of this. And their dreams keep them alive from one miserable day to the next.

At nine-thirty, Sergeant Packer was looking for Sam. Packer had two guards with him and some chains. Sam pointed at the chains, and asked, "What are they for?"

"Security, Sam. We're taking you to the law library. Your lawyer wants to meet you there."

When Sam's legs had been chained together, he walked stiffly out of the cell with Packer at his side and guards following.

The law library was a small room with a good collection of current law books. It was used only by death row inmates. Sam had been there many times during the past nine years. The guards removed his chains at the door.

"You've got two hours," Packer said.

Sam entered the library and closed the door behind him. Adam stood at the other end of the conference table, waiting for his client. Sam stood there in his red jumpsuit. There was a slightly awkward pause.

"Hello, Sam," Adam said, walking toward him.

"Mornin'."

"Have you seen the paper?" Adam slid the morning paper across the table. Sam sat down and began to read. There was a long article about them and pictures of himself and Adam. The story told how Sam Cayhall's new lawyer was in fact his long-lost grandson. The reporter had managed to find some family background, but the article did not mention Sam's daughter in Memphis so Lee was spared for the moment.

Sam said, "Stay away from the press. They lie and they make mistakes. I don't want this to happen again."

Adam reached into his briefcase and pulled out some papers. "I have a great idea about how to save your life."

"I'm listening."

"I've got a theory, a new claim which I intend to file on Monday. Mississippi is one of only five states still using the gas chamber, right?"

"That's right."

"And Mississippi passed a law in 1984 giving a man the choice of dying by lethal injection or in the gas chamber. But the new law applies only to those found guilty after July 1, 1984. It doesn't apply to you."

"That's right. I don't get a choice."

"One of the reasons for the new law was to make the killings less cruel. I've studied the history behind the law and there was a lot of discussion of problems the state's had with gas chamber executions. Lethal injections raise fewer legal problems. The state has in effect said that gas chamber executions should no longer be used, because the gas chamber is a cruel way to kill people."

Sam nodded slowly. "Keep going," he said.

"We attack the gas chamber as a method of execution. I know there were problems with Teddy Doyle Meeks and Maynard Tole."

Sam laughed bitterly. "Problems? You could say that."

"How much do you know?"

"They died within fifty yards of me." Sam leaned forward.

34

"Meeks was the first execution in Mississippi in ten years, and they didn't know what they were doing. Everything went wrong. Have you seen the chamber?"

"Not yet."

"There's not much room inside — just a wooden seat with a metal bowl directly under it. The executioner is in a little room off to the side. He has some acid in a container which he sends along a tube to the bowl. When the bowl fills with acid, he pulls a lever and cyanide tablets drop from a little bag into the bowl. This causes the gas, which causes death. It should be painless and quick."

"What went wrong in Meeks' case?"

"The executioner was drunk. His first try with the acid didn't work. He placed the container into the tube, pulled a lever, and everyone waited for Meeks to die. Nothing happened. The executioner mixed up some more acid, put the new container in the tube and pulled the lever. This time the acid landed where it was supposed to — in the bowl under the chair. The executioner pulled the second lever, dropping the cyanide tablets into the acid, and the gas rose upward to where Meeks was holding his breath. When Meeks finally sucked in a nose full of it, he started shaking violently, and this went on for a long time. For some reason, there's a metal pole that runs from the top of the chamber to the bottom, and it's directly behind the chair. Just about the time Meeks went still and everybody thought he was dead, his head started banging backward and forward, striking this pole. His eyes rolled back, his lips were wide open, liquid was running from his mouth. It took a long time for him to die. It was sick."

Sam's version of Meeks' death was very similar to the accounts given by the eyewitnesses. There was no doubt that the man had suffered greatly.

"What about Maynard Tole?" Adam asked.

"He was an African who'd killed people in a robbery, and he suffered just the same as Meeks. They found him a new executioner. The gas hit Tole and he started shaking, banging his head on the pole just like Meeks, except Tole obviously had a harder head because it went on and on. Finally Naifeh got really anxious because the boy wouldn't die and things were getting messy, so they actually made the witnesses leave the witness room."

"I read that it took ten minutes for him to die. You see my point, Sam? It's horrible. We attack the method. We find witnesses who'll give evidence about these executions and then we try to find a judge to rule against the gas chamber."

"Then what? Do we ask for lethal injection? What's the point? Seems kind of silly for me to say I prefer not to die in the chamber, but lethal injection will do just fine. I'll be dead, right?"

"True. But we buy ourselves some time. We'll attack the gas chamber, get a temporary delay, then take it through the higher courts. We could make it last for years."

Sam turned and walked slowly to Adam's end of the table and took a seat. "I like this idea," he said quietly.

"Good. Let's get to work. I want to find more cases like the ones you've told me about. Let's dig up every gas chamber execution that ever went wrong. And make a list of people that might give evidence about Meeks and Tole."

Sam was already on his feet, pulling books from shelves.

◆

From the air, all that could be seen were two ordinary-looking wooden houses, set among the rolling wheat fields. The security wire fences that surrounded the site were hidden with hedges. But below, deep in the hills, were two tunnels with elevators leading deep underground, caves connected by underground

36

passages. One had a printing press, another was full of weapons. Three were living spaces. One was a library. The largest was the central hall where members gathered for speeches, films, and meetings.

The newspapers that arrived each day were first read by a man named Roland Forchin. He lived in this secret hiding place most of the time. If a story in one of the papers caught his attention, he would mark it and later make a copy of it and give it to the computer desk. Mostly he collected stories about right-wing groups similar to his.

This particular morning was different. He first smelled trouble when he saw a picture of Sam Cayhall in a San Francisco daily. The news was that the oldest man on death row in America would now be represented by his grandson. Roland read it three times. After an hour, he'd read the same story in several different papers.

Roland had followed the case of Sam Cayhall for many years. It was the type of case that interested his organization, but he had a more personal interest in the case. He wanted Sam Cayhall dead. One of Roland's other names, known only to himself, was Rollie Wedge. He had left the United States in 1967, after the Kramer bombing, and since then had lived in many different countries.

He had been dreaming of Cayhall's death for twenty-three years. He and Sam shared a secret. When Sam was finally executed, Roland would no longer have to fear that secret would ever be revealed. This kid worried him. Roland hadn't managed to trace Sam's son and his family. He knew about the daughter in Memphis, but the son had disappeared. And now this nice-looking, well-educated young lawyer had arrived from nowhere to save his grandfather. Over the years, Sam had refused to say anything. If he was going to talk, it would be now.

Roland would have to go to Memphis.

Chapter 6 Questions of Guilt

Calico Rock was a small town on a high bank above the river, two hours' drive from Memphis. Three fishing docks lined the east bank. Adam parked by the river and walked to the first dock. A row of empty boats was tied up alongside. A smell of gasoline and oil came from a single gas pump.

A huge man appeared from a back room.

"I'm looking for Wyn Lettner."

"I'm Wyn Lettner." He had a deep voice and a pleasant smile.

Adam held out a hand, and said, "I'm Adam Hall."

Lettner shook the hand hard. "What can I do for you?"

Fortunately there was no one else on the dock. "Well, I'm a lawyer, and I represent Sam Cayhall."

The smile grew. "Quite a challenge."

"I guess so. I'd like to talk about Sam."

Lettner was suddenly serious. "I saw it in the papers, son. I know Sam's your grandfather. Must be tough on you. So what can I tell you?"

"Garner Goodman gave me your name. Told me you were the FBI agent in charge of the Kramer case. He says you know more about the Kramer bombing than anyone."

"I talked to Garner Goodman a few times. It was years ago. You like to fish?" he asked, admiring the river.

"No. Never been."

"Let's go for a ride. We can talk when we get there."

Lettner stepped down from the dock into a boat, which shook violently. "Come on," he shouted. Adam jumped in nervously. Lettner started the engine, and Calico Rock was soon behind them. The noise of the engine prevented conversation.

The boat slowed finally under some trees, and Lettner turned off the engine and began to fish. "Listen, son, I'm not going to tell you anything useful, you understand?"

"Why not?"

"Some things I can talk about, some I can't. And Sam was of no concern to us, at least not at first. He wasn't active in the really nasty stuff. The FBI got involved when some civil rights workers disappeared. We spread money all over the place, and before long we had people inside the Klan giving us information. We made some arrests, and it made us look good, but the violence continued. We spread around more money, got more information. We had ways of getting people to talk. In the end it worked. They were all afraid to do anything much. The violence had slowed until Dogan decided to go after the Jews. That surprised us, I admit. We had no clue."

"Why not?"

"Because Dogan had learned the hard way that his own people would talk to us, so he decided to operate with a small, quiet unit."

"Unit? As in more than one person?"

Lettner laughed but did not answer.

"Sam wasn't alone when he bombed the Kramer office, was he?" Adam continued.

"You think he had some help?"

"Of course he had help. Sam had no knowledge of explosives. When the FBI searched Sam's house, they found nothing, right? No trace of dynamite, fuses, timers?"

"That's correct."

"Did you know about Sam before then?" Adam asked.

"His name was in our records. His father was in the Klan, and a brother or two. But they seemed harmless."

"Then how do you explain Sam's sudden move to violence?"

"It wasn't that sudden, OK? He had killed before."

"Are you sure?"

"You heard me. He shot and killed one of his black employees

39

in the early fifties. There may have been another killing, too. Another black victim."

"I'd rather not hear this."

"Ask him. See if he has the courage to admit it to his grandson. He was a violent man, son. Don't forget that."

Lettner decided the fish had moved elsewhere and started the engine again. They stopped on a stretch of still water below a high bank.

"About Sam," Lettner began eventually. "He's not a bad guy. I don't want him to be executed. And like you, we always thought he had a partner."

"Why?" Adam asked.

"For the same reasons. Sam had no history with bombs. He didn't seem the type to do it alone."

"So who's the man?"

"I honestly don't know. We were tough with anyone that might give us information, but only Dogan knew, and he wasn't telling anybody."

"So why didn't Dogan name him when he decided to give evidence against Sam?"

"Would you talk about a terrorist who was still out there?"

Adam gave that some thought.

Lettner continued, "There are a few more things that maybe I should tell you. You know that Dogan died a year after he gave evidence against Sam?"

"I had heard that."

"He and his wife were killed when their house blew up. Some kind of gas leak. Well, we never believed it was an accident."

"How does this affect Sam?"

"It doesn't affect Sam, but it might affect you. Who knew the details of the bombing?"

"Sam. Jeremiah Dogan."

"Right. Who was their lawyer in the first two trials?"

"Clovis Brazelton."

"Brazelton also died. In a plane crash. He was flying back from the Coast one night when the plane disappeared. They found his body in a tree. The weather was clear. They guessed at some kind of engine failure."

"Another strange death. What are you trying to tell me?"

"It's possible the deaths were the work of the same person, Sam's mysterious partner in the bombing. Sam's the only witness left. If Sam starts talking, the man's in trouble. And you're the one trying to find out the truth."

"You think I might be in danger."

"There's possible danger, Adam. Be careful."

I've got to keep this guy away from Lee, Adam thought. "Thanks, I guess," he said.

"Let's get back and have a beer."

◆

Things were not going well in the kitchen when Adam arrived back at Lee's. She'd confessed to being a terrible cook, and now she was proving it. Pots and pans were scattered along the countertops. She laughed and said there was a frozen pizza if matters got worse.

"Have you seen the Memphis paper?" she asked him.

"No. Should I?"

"Yes. It's over there." She nodded to the corner.

Adam picked up the latest *Memphis Press*. On the front page of the second section, he suddenly met his own smiling face. It was a photo taken when he was a law student at Michigan. This new story covered half a page, and his photo was joined by many others.

A history of the case took up an entire column, then the story

41

moved to the present situation. There were interviews. McAllister, of course, had plenty to say. He had lived with the Kramer horror for twenty-three years, thinking about it every day of his life since it happened. It had been his honor and privilege to prosecute Sam Cayhall and bring the killer to justice, and only the execution could close this awful chapter of Mississippi's history. No, after much thought, a pardon was impossible. It just wouldn't be fair to the little Kramer boys. And on and on.

Elliot Kramer, Marvin's father, now seventy-seven and still working, was described as fit and healthy. He was also very bitter. He blamed the Klan and Sam Cayhall not only for killing his two grandsons, but also for Marvin's death. He'd been waiting twenty-three years for Sam to be executed, and it couldn't come too soon. He wanted to be there at the execution and look Cayhall in the eyes when they killed him.

Adam folded the paper. He suddenly had a knot in his stomach. As the lawyer expected to save Sam's life, it was frightening to see his enemies so eager for the final battle. At this moment he felt completely hopeless.

◆

Sam threw his cigarette on the floor and leaned forward. The lines tightened in the corners of his eyes and across his forehead. "So this is it. Time for our Eddie talk."

Adam repeated his question. "What happened to my father? Why didn't he become like you?"

"This is a waste of time."

"Don't be a coward, Sam. Tell me about Eddie. Where did you go wrong? Did you teach him to hate little black kids? Did you teach him how to build bombs?"

"Eddie didn't know I was in the Klan until he was in high school."

"Why not? Surely you weren't ashamed of it."

"Eddie was different."

"You mean, he didn't hate?"

Sam continued. "Eddie was a tender child. He was like his mother. There was a black family on our place. The Lincolns. Joe Lincoln had worked for us for many years. One of the boys, Quince, was the same age as Eddie, and they were best of friends. When Eddie started school, he got real upset because he rode one bus and his African friend rode another. He was always asking questions about why the Africans in Ford County were so poor, and lived in bad houses, and didn't have nice clothes, and had so many children. He suffered over them, and that made him different. I tried to explain things to him."

"Such as?"

"Such as the need to keep the races separate. There's nothing wrong with keeping Africans in their place. Eddie left home when he was eighteen."

"Did you miss him?"

"Not at first, I guess. We were fighting a lot. He knew I was in the Klan by then, and he said he hated the sight of me."

"You thought more of the Klan than of your own son?"

Sam stared at the floor. "He was a sweet kid," he said quietly. "We had an old boat and used to fish, that was our big thing together. Then he grew up and didn't like me. He was ashamed of me, and of course it hurt." He looked up at Adam. "What kind of father was he?"

"I don't know. That's a hard question, Sam."

"Why?"

"Because of the way he died. I was mad at him for a long time after his death, and I didn't understand how he could leave us, how he could decide we didn't need him anymore. And after I learned the truth, I was mad at him for lying to me all those

43

years, for changing my name and running away. It was terribly confusing for a young kid. Still is."

"Are you still angry?"

"Not really. I try to remember the good things about Eddie. I guess he was a good man, a good father who just had this dark, strange side to him."

"Tell me about his death. How did it happen?"

Adam waited a long time before answering. "He was going through a bad time. He'd been in his room for three weeks, hiding from the world. Mother kept telling us that he was getting better, soon he'd come out. We believed her. He picked a day when she was at work and Carmen was at a friend's house, a day when he knew I'd be the first one home. I found him lying on the floor of my bedroom, still holding the gun. One shot in his forehead. There was a neat circle of blood, and a typed note beside him. The note was addressed *Dear Adam*. It said he loved me, that he was sorry, that he wanted me to take care of the girls, and that maybe one day I would understand. He asked me to clean up the mess and call the police. Don't touch the gun, he said. And hurry, before the girls get home." Adam cleared his throat and looked at the floor.

"And so I did what he said, and I waited for the police. We were alone for fifteen minutes, just the two of us. He was lying on the floor, and I was lying on my bed looking down at him. I started crying and crying, asking him why. There was my dad, the only dad I would ever have. I heard voices, and suddenly the room was filled with police."

Sam was leaning on his elbows, one hand over his eyes. There were just a couple more things Adam wanted to say.

"Lee stayed with us after the funeral and told me everything. I couldn't stop thinking about you and the Kramer bombing. It took about a year for me to figure out why Eddie killed himself

44

when he did. He'd been hiding in his room during your trial, and he killed himself when it ended."

Sam removed his hand and stared at Adam with wet eyes. "So you blame me for his death, right, Adam? That's what you really want to say?"

"No, I don't blame you entirely."

"Then how much? Eighty percent? Ninety percent? How much of it's my fault?"

"I don't know, Sam. Why don't you tell me?"

"Just add my son's name to the list, is that what you want? The Kramer twins, their father, then Eddie. That's four I've killed, right? Anyone else you want to add?"

"How many more are out there?"

"Dead bodies?"

"Yes. Dead bodies. I've heard the rumors."

Sam jumped to his feet and walked to the end of the room. "I'm tired of this conversation!" he shouted. "And I'm tired of you! Here I am twenty-three days away from the chamber, and all you want to do is talk about dead people. Just get out of here!"

Chapter 7   My Dear Sweet Father

Death penalty appeals usually go on for years. No one is in a hurry. When a date for an execution has been set, however, decisions can be made with amazing speed. Adam had a taste of this quick justice on Monday afternoon. The Mississippi Supreme Court took one look at his appeal, and turned it down. Their decision was quickly sent on to Judge F. Flynn Slattery at the federal district court in Jackson.

At six on Tuesday morning, Adam jumped into his car and

raced to Jackson. At nine, he entered the federal courthouse and was told to return at eleven.

Although he arrived on time, it was obvious that a meeting had been in progress for some time. Slattery sat at one end, with piles of paper in front of him. Closest to him sat the governor, David McAllister. The Attorney General, Steve Roxburgh, sat in the middle. Around them their side of the table was crowded with young white men in navy suits, the state's legal representatives. The room was immediately silent as Adam approached the table. Slattery rose and introduced himself. Adam took a seat on the opposite side, feeling lonely.

"Hope we're not going too quickly for you, Mr. Hall," Slattery said. "When do you expect to officially file your appeal here in federal court?"

"Today, Your Honor," Adam said nervously.

"When can the state respond?" the judge asked the Attorney General.

"Tomorrow morning. If the appeal here raises the same issues as those raised in the supreme court."

"They're the same," Adam said.

"Get the appeal filed today. The state will file its response tomorrow. I'll consider it at the weekend and issue a judgment on Monday. I'm trying to move things along for you."

"Thank you," Adam said.

Slattery wrote something, then studied it. He gave it to his clerk, who raced off to do something else with it. His Honor looked again at young Adam. "Now, Mr. Hall, this execution is planned to take place in twenty-two days, and I would like to know if this court can expect any additional appeals on behalf of Mr. Cayhall. I know this is an unusual request, but it's an unusual situation. I would like us to work together."

In other words, Your Honor, you want to make absolutely sure that there are no delays, Adam thought. Sam had a right to file anything at any time, and Adam could not make any promises. "I really can't say, Your Honor. Not now."

"Surely you'll file all the usual last-minute appeals," Roxburgh said, and the pack of young lawyers grinned.

"Very well, gentlemen," Slattery ended. "I suggest you stay by your telephones Sunday night and Monday morning. I'll call as soon as I've made a decision."

The group on the other side of the table broke up. Adam offered his goodbyes and left the room. Out in the hallway, someone called his name. It was McAllister.

"Can we talk?" McAllister asked.

"What about?"

"Just five minutes, OK?"

"Somewhere private then."

"Sure," McAllister said. They stepped inside a small empty courtroom. The governor leaned against a wall. He was under forty and looked good for his age. "How's Sam?" he asked, pretending deep concern.

Adam sat his briefcase on the floor. "Oh, he's wonderful. I'll tell him you asked. You're trying to kill him. How can you be worried about his health?"

"I just heard a rumor that he wasn't too well."

"Sam hates you, OK? His health is not too good, but he'll survive for another three weeks."

"Hate is nothing new for Sam, you know."

"Look, Governor, I have a signed contract with my client that forbids me to talk to you. You're the reason he's on death row. If he knew we were talking now, I'd be on my way back to Chicago."

"But if we can't talk, then how do we discuss the issue of clemency?"

"I don't know. I haven't reached that point yet."

"I'm not sure he should die."

Adam started to say something, then realized the importance of the governor's last words.

"How much has he told you about the Kramer bombing?" McAllister asked.

"He says he's told me everything."

"But you have doubts?"

"Yes."

"So do I. I always thought that Sam must have had a partner in the bombing. Have you asked him that?"

Adam paused for a second. "I really can't discuss what Sam and I have talked about. It's confidential."

"Of course it is. But what if Sam didn't plan to kill anyone? Sam was there, right in the middle of it. But what if someone else actually *planned* to commit murder?"

"Then Sam isn't as guilty as we think."

"Right. He's certainly not innocent, but not guilty enough to be executed either." The governor slipped a hand in his pocket and pulled out a business card. "Two phone numbers on the back. My private office number and my home number. All phone calls are confidential."

Adam took the card and looked at the numbers.

"I couldn't live with myself if I failed to pardon a man who didn't deserve to die," McAllister said as he walked to the door. "Give me a call, but don't wait until it's too late."

♦

Rollie Wedge waited patiently at the table of a sidewalk café until the black Saab appeared, then turned into a nearby parking garage. He watched Adam walk along the sidewalk and enter the building.

The entrance was empty as Wedge looked at the information

sign. Kravitz and Bane had the third and fourth floors. He rode one of the elevators, alone, to the third floor. There was a receptionist at a desk. He was just going to ask her something when the phone rang and she became occupied with it, so he went back to the elevator and went up to the fourth floor. There was no receptionist this time, but the doors were locked. On a wall to the right was a coded entry display with nine numbered buttons.

Wedge stepped back to wait by the stairs. An elevator opened, and a young man came out with a box under one arm. He walked toward the Kravitz and Bane doors. He did not notice as Wedge came up behind him. He began to enter the code. Seven, seven, three. Wedge was inches behind, watching over his shoulder and memorizing the code.

After leaving the building, Wedge drove until he came to a section of the city filled with government housing. He pulled into a driveway beside Auburn House and was stopped by a uniformed guard. He was just turning round, he explained, lost again. As he backed onto the street, he made sure Lee Booth's red Jaguar was parked there.

Wedge drove toward the river, and parked at an abandoned factory. He walked toward a row of luxury houses surrounded by a fence and with a guard in a gatehouse. He crawled round the fence and along by the river, keeping out of sight, then stopped at the seventh house, where he swung up onto the patio. The glass door into the kitchen was locked, a rather simple lock that gave him no problems. He knew there would be a security alarm system, so he stepped inside carefully.

The guard at the gate immediately noticed the alarm signal. He looked at the red light flashing at Number 7, home of Lee Booth. He opened the key drawer and selected one for Number 7, then left the gatehouse and walked quickly across the parking lot to check Mrs. Booth's unit. His gun was in his hand, just in case.

Rollie Wedge stepped into the gatehouse and saw the open key drawer. He took a set marked for Number 7, with a card listing the alarm code and instructions, and also took keys for Numbers 8 and 13, just to confuse the police.

◆

Adam and Lee had lunch in Clanton, and then left the town on a county highway running through small, neat farms in pretty, hilly countryside. Adam drove and Lee pointed the way. They turned onto a smaller road that led deep into the country, and finally stopped in front of an abandoned white frame house. The garden was overgrown and the drive leading to the house was full of holes.

"The Cayhall house," she whispered, and they sat in the car and looked at the sad little building.

"What happened to it?" Adam finally asked.

"Oh, it was a good house. The people were a disappointment, though. I lived here for eighteen years, and I couldn't wait to leave it."

The car was hot, and Adam opened his door. "I want to look around," he said, getting out. They went up the drive and stood by the door, looking at the rotten wood.

"I'm not going in there," Lee said firmly. Adam walked along the front of the house, looking in through the windows while Lee followed him. The backyard was shaded by old trees and stretched for an eighth of a mile down a slight slope. Lee walked over to a tree. "This was my tree," she said, looking up at the branches. "My own tree." Her voice shook a little.

"It's a great tree."

"Wonderful for climbing. I'd spend hours here, sitting in the branches. I'd climb halfway up, and no one could see me." She closed her eyes.

"This is where it happened," she said after a moment. She fought back tears. Adam said nothing.

"This is the story of Daddy killing a black man. His name was Joe Lincoln, and he lived down the road there with his family." She nodded along a dirt track that ran down to the woods. "He had about a dozen kids."

"Quince Lincoln?"

"Yeah. How do you know about him?"

"Sam mentioned his name the other day. He said Quince and Eddie were good friends as kids."

"I don't suppose he told you about his father. Joe worked here on the farm for us. He was a good man with a big family, very poor. One day the boys were playing here in the backyard; it was summertime and we weren't in school. They got into an argument over a small toy, a model soldier. It was lost, and Eddie accused Quince of stealing it. Typical boy stuff, you know. They were eight or nine years old. Daddy happened to walk past, and Eddie ran to him and told him that Quince had stolen the toy. Quince denied it. Sam exploded and called Quince all sorts of names. Quince started crying. He kept saying he didn't have the soldier. Sam took hold of the boy and started hitting him. Quince finally pulled free and ran home. Eddie ran into our house, and Sam followed. A moment later, Sam stepped outside again, with a stick. He sat on the steps and waited. The Lincoln house was not far away, and within a few minutes Joe came running out of the trees there with Quince right behind him. As he got close to the house, Daddy shouted over his shoulder, 'Eddie! Come here! Watch me whip this dirty Negro!'"

Lee began walking very slowly to the house, then stopped. "When Joe was right about here, he stopped and looked at Sam. He said, 'Quince says you hit him, Mr. Sam.' An argument started, and they began to fight. They fell to the ground and fought like

51

cats. Eddie was standing watching it all. Quince stood there and shouted at his father. Sam ran to the steps and picked up the stick. He beat Joe in the face and head until he fell to his knees. Joe could hardly move. He looked at Quince and shouted for him to run and get his shotgun. Quince ran off. Sam stopped beating Joe, and turned to Eddie. 'Go get my shotgun,' he said. Eddie didn't move, and Daddy shouted at him again. Eddie went inside. Joe tried to get up, but Sam knocked him down again. Eddie returned with a shotgun, and Daddy made him go inside."

Lee sat on the steps and hid her face in her hands.

"Finish it, please," Adam said.

She wiped her eyes. "Joe was just over there. He got to his feet, and he turned and saw Daddy with the gun. There was no sign of Quince. Then my dear sweet father slowly raised the gun, looked round to see if anyone was watching, and fired. Just like that. Joe fell and never moved. He was dead."

"You saw this happen, didn't you?"

"Yes, I did."

"Where were you?"

"Over there," she nodded. "In my tree. Hidden from the world. Sam couldn't see me. Quince appeared after a few minutes. He'd heard the shot, and he was crying. He ran to his father, and his shirt was soon covered in blood. He held his father's head next to him, blood was everywhere, and he made strange crying sounds, like an animal." She looked up at the tree. "And there I was, sitting up there like a little bird, crying too. I hated my father so much just then."

"Later, Eddie found me in our secret hiding place in the woods. He reached in his pocket and pulled something out. It was the little toy soldier he'd accused Quince of stealing. He'd found it under his bed, and so he decided then that everything was his fault. And I blamed myself because I should've shouted at Daddy before he fired the gun. I don't think he would have killed Joe with his daughter watching. We swore that we would keep it a secret, Eddie and I. He promised he would never tell anyone that I'd witnessed the killing, and I promised I would never tell anyone that he'd found the soldier. But we both carried that guilt around until we were grown. I don't think he ever recovered from it."

Adam bent over gently and took Lee's arm. "Let's go, Lee. I've heard enough for one day."

They got back to the car without a word, and drove out to the highway. Lee asked him to stop at a store. She returned with a six-pack of beer. "What's this?" Adam said.

"Just a couple," she said. "For my nerves. Don't let me drink more than two, OK? Only two."

"I don't think you should, Lee."

Adam sped away from the store. Lee emptied two bottles in fifteen minutes, then went to sleep. Adam concentrated on the road. He had a sudden desire to leave Mississippi, and to see the bright lights of Memphis.

Chapter 8   A Cruel Way to Die

On Sunday, Adam was alone in the office, but found it difficult to concentrate. He was worried about Lee and he hated Sam. He had not seen his client for six days.

Adam struggled with horrible pictures in his mind. He saw Quince Lincoln bent over his father's body and heard the shocked whispers of Eddie and Lee as they blamed themselves for the awful thing that Sam had done.

The phone rang. He recognized the voice of Judge Slattery. "Mr. Hall, I've carefully considered this matter, and I'm denying your appeal," he said.

"Yes, sir," Adam said.

"You'll need to send it on to the Fifth Circuit in New Orleans as soon as possible, you know."

"I'm working on it now, Your Honor."

"Good day, Mr. Hall."

Adam got back to work. Sam had sixteen days to live.

◆

Adam was waiting for Sam in the law library the next day. They shook hands. "Where've you been?" asked Sam.

"Busy," Adam said. As he looked at Sam, he tried not to think about Joe Lincoln. "I guess you've heard about our latest defeat," he said. "A rather quick loss, but I've already referred it to the Fifth Circuit Court of Appeals."

"What else can we do?"

"Several things. I met the governor at the judge's offices. He wanted to talk in private. Said he had doubts about your guilt."

"You promised not to talk to him. You signed an agreement with me forbidding any contact with that fool."

"Relax, Sam. It was a chance meeting. He's open to the idea of clemency."

"He told you this? Why? I don't believe it."

"I don't know why, Sam. But we must consider it."

"No. The answer is no. I do not give my permission for a clemency hearing. He will not change his mind. It's all a show for the public."

"What do you want to do then, Sam? You think you know about the law – tell me what you want to do."

"Well, I've been thinking. The appeal to the Fifth Circuit doesn't look promising. There's not a lot left."

"Except to attack your lawyer at the last trial, Benjamin Keyes. Say he didn't do a good job."

"Keyes did a fine job for me at trial, and he was almost a friend. I hate to do it."

"It's standard in death cases, Sam. You go after the lawyer who represented you at the final trial and claim that he didn't represent you effectively. It should've been done years ago."

"Goodman wanted me to, but I said no. I guess I was wrong."

Adam was taking notes. "I think Keyes made a mistake at the trial when he didn't let you give evidence yourself."

"I wanted to talk to the jury, you know. I wanted to tell them that I did in fact plant the bomb, but I didn't intend to kill anyone. That's the truth, Adam."

"You wanted to give evidence, but your lawyer said no."

"That's the way it happened."

"I'll file first thing in the morning."

Sam began walking about. Adam watched him.

"Lee and I went to Clanton. She took me to her childhood home."

"It's still there?"

"Yeah, it's abandoned. The house is falling down and the garden is overgrown. We walked around the place. She told me stories about her childhood. Talked about Eddie."

Sam returned to his seat. "Did she tell you about Eddie's little friend, Quince Lincoln?"

Adam nodded slowly. "Yes, she did."

"And about his father, Joe?"

"She told me the story."

"It's all true. How did you feel when she told you?"

"I hated you."

Sam crossed his arms and stared at the wall. "I've wished a thousand times that it hadn't happened."

"I promised Lee that I wouldn't mention it, Sam. I'm sorry," said Adam.

"Joe Lincoln was a good man. I've often wondered what happened to Ruby and Quince and the rest of the kids. I hope they're happy when I'm dead."

◆

The urgent phone call was from the clerk of the Fifth Circuit Court of Appeals in New Orleans. He said that the appeal attacking the gas chamber had been received on Monday. It had been given to a three-judge team, and the judges wanted to hear from both sides in person. Could Adam be in New Orleans at 1 p.m. tomorrow, Friday?

Adam almost dropped the phone. "Of course," he said after a slight hesitation. The clerk asked Adam if he'd ever argued before the Fifth Circuit before.

"Are you kidding?" Adam thought. "A year ago I was still studying for my exams." He said "no," and the clerk said he would immediately send Adam a copy of the court's rules.

Adam called Goodman with the news, and to get his advice. Goodman assured him that he could handle the arguments. "Just be prepared," he said. Adam put down the phone and started work.

He worked until dark, then went back to Lee's. The apartment was dark, and there was no sign of movement or life. Her bedroom door was slightly open. He tapped on it. "Lee," he called gently. "Are you all right?"

"Yes, dear," she said. "Come in. I've been ill, but I'm feeling a little better already. The doctor said it'll only last a few days."

Adam entered the room, and caught the strong smell of alcohol. He wanted to cry. "Does your doctor know you're drinking?" he asked.

There was a pause. "I haven't been drinking," she said.

"I can smell it, Lee. You're not fooling anyone."

56

Lee pulled her legs up to her chest. She sat for a long time. The apartment was quiet. Finally she spoke.

"I think we'll be happier when my father's dead. God knows he deserves to die."

"Why does he deserve it? He's sorry about Joe Lincoln."

"It wasn't only Joe Lincoln, you know. Has Sam told you about the lynching?"

Adam closed his eyes. "No," he whispered.

"I didn't think so."

"I don't want to hear it, Lee."

"Yes, you do. You came down here full of questions about the family. You wanted to know everything."

"I've heard enough," he said.

"Mother told me the story," she said quietly. "She said she'd heard rumors about it for years. Long before they married she knew he'd helped lynch a young black man."

"Please, Lee."

"The story was that a black kid had forced a white girl to have sex with him. Many people doubted whether he'd really forced her. Sam was fifteen or so at the time. A group of men went down to the jail, got the black kid, and took him out in the woods. Sam's father, of course, was one of the leaders, and his brothers were involved."

"That's enough, Lee."

"They beat him with a leather whip, then hung him from a tree. My dear father was right in the middle of it. He couldn't really deny it, you know, because somebody took a picture."

"A photograph?"

"Yeah. A few years later the photo found its way into a book about the history of Negroes in the Deep South. My mother had a copy of the book."

"And Sam's in the photograph?"

"Sure. Smiling from ear to ear. They're standing under the tree and the black guy's feet are hanging just above their heads. Everybody's having fun."

"Where's the book?"

"Over there in the drawer. I've kept it with all the other family photographs. I thought you might want to see it."

"No. I *don't* want to see it."

"You wanted to know about your family. Well, there they are. All sorts of Cayhalls at their very best."

"Stop it, Lee."

"There were other lynchings, you know."

"Shut up, Lee, OK? I don't want to hear any more." Adam jumped up. "You're drunk, and you need to sleep."

◆

At ten minutes before one the next day, Adam walked through the massive oak doors of the West Courtroom at the Fifth Circuit Court of Appeals in New Orleans. Attorney General Roxburgh and his assistants were already there preparing for battle. Adam breathed deeply and tried to relax. He kept telling himself that the judges couldn't kill him, they could only embarrass him – and even that wouldn't last long.

A court official appeared from behind the bench and announced that the court was going to begin its proceedings. He was followed by three figures in black – Judges McNeely, Robichaux, and Judy. They sat in their massive leather chairs high up on the dark, shiny, oak bench and looked down on the courtroom. The case of *State of Mississippi against Sam Cayhall* was called, and the attorneys came to the front of the room. Judge Judy asked Mr. Adam Hall from Chicago if he was ready to proceed. Adam stood there, his knees rubber-like, his voice high and nervous, and he said that yes, he was ready to go.

The green light beside Adam came on, which meant that he

had exactly twenty minutes to speak. For several minutes he repeated the arguments he'd already made in writing.

"Mr. Hall, we're just hearing the points you've already sent to us," Judy said crossly. "We're quite capable of reading."

"Yes, Your Honor," Adam said. He then moved on to discuss the effect of cyanide gas on laboratory rats, a new subject. The experiments had been carried out a year ago by some scientists in Sweden to prove that humans do not die immediately when they breathe in the poison.

The rats' lungs and hearts stopped and started for several minutes. The gas burst blood vessels throughout their bodies, including their brains. Their muscles moved uncontrollably. The obvious point of the study was to show that the rats suffered a great deal. On average, it took ten minutes for death to occur. The judges seemed to be not only listening, but enjoying this discussion of dying rats.

"Now, let me understand you correctly," Robichaux interrupted. "You don't want your client to die in the gas chamber because it's a cruel way to go, but are you telling us you don't mind if he's executed by lethal injection?"

"No, Your Honor. That's not what I'm saying. I do not want my client executed by any method. All methods are offensive, but lethal injection seems to be the least horrible. There's no doubt the gas chamber is a cruel way to die."

"Worse than being bombed? Blown up by dynamite?"

A heavy silence fell over the courtroom. Adam struggled for an appropriate response. He said firmly, "We're talking about methods of execution, Your Honor, not the crimes that send men to death row."

"Perhaps your client shouldn't have bombed buildings?"

"Of course not. But he was found guilty of his crime, and now he faces death in the gas chamber. Our point is that the chamber is a cruel way to execute people."

"But you like the idea of lethal injection?"

"I didn't say I like it. I said it was less cruel than other methods."

Justice McNeely interrupted and asked, "Mr. Hall, why did Mississippi switch from the gas chamber to lethal injection?"

Adam sensed immediately that McNeely was a friend. "Almost every state with a gas chamber or an electric chair has switched to lethal injection. The reason is obvious. It is an easier way to die."

"So the State has effectively admitted that there is a better way to execute people."

"Yes, sir. But the law took effect in 1984, and does not therefore apply to Sam Cayhall." The yellow light next to Adam came on, showing that his time was almost at an end. "So, Your Honor, I'm asking the court to reconsider its decision on this issue. Thank you." He walked back to his seat.

Roxburgh spoke next, and was well prepared. He tried a few jokes about rats and the crimes they commit, but it was a poor effort at humor. McNeely asked him similar questions about why the states were rushing to use lethal injections. Roxburgh gave examples of many cases where various courts had supported death by gas, electricity, hanging, and shooting. The law was on his side, and he made the most of it.

Judge Judy talked about the urgency of the matter, and promised a decision within days. Everyone rose, and the three judges disappeared from the bench. Adam shook hands with the Attorney General and got through the doors before the reporters could stop him. He had done his best for Sam, with twelve days to go.

Chapter 9   A Parchman Sunrise

The temperature outside was 102, and not much cooler inside the visitors' room. It was Saturday, and Adam was dressed in jeans and a very light cotton shirt.

"I understand you were in New Orleans yesterday," said Sam. "Tell me about it."

"The Fifth Circuit called Thursday, and said they wanted to hear from me on Friday. I went down, impressed them with my brilliance, and flew back to Memphis this morning. We'll get their judgment soon."

"Which judges?"

"Judy, Robichaux, and McNeely."

Sam thought about the names for a moment. "McNeely's an old fighter who'll help us. Judy's a Republican appointee. I doubt she'll help. I'm not familiar with Robichaux. Where's he from?"

"Southern Louisiana. He's pretty hard. He won't help."

"Then we'll lose by two to one. I thought you said you impressed them."

"We haven't lost yet." Adam was surprised to hear Sam speak with such familiarity about the individual judges. But he'd been studying the court for many years.

"Where's the ineffective representation claim, Adam?"

"Still in district court here. A few days behind the other."

"Let's file something else, OK, quick. I've got eleven days. There's a calendar on my wall, and I spend at least three hours a day staring at it. When I wake up in the morning I make a big X over the date for the day before. I've got a circle around August 8. My Xs are getting close to the circle. Do something."

"I'm developing a new theory of attack. I think we can prove you're mentally unbalanced."

"I've been considering that."

"You're old. You're too calm about this. Something must be wrong inside your head. You're unable to understand the reason for your execution."

"We've been reading the same cases."

61

"Goodman knows an expert who will say anything for a fee. We'll bring him down here to examine you."

"Wonderful. Let's do it. Let's file everything we can."

They were both sweating, and Adam needed fresh air. There was one more thing.

"Listen, Sam, this is not a pleasant subject, but we need to address it. You're going to die one of these days. It might be on August 8, or it might be five years from now. Your family, Lee and I, need to make some burial arrangements. It can't be done overnight."

Sam stared at the screen and thought for a few minutes.

"Your grandmother was a fine lady, Adam. I'm sorry you didn't know her. She deserved better than me. I caused her a lot of suffering, and she bore it well. Bury me next to her, and maybe I can tell her I'm sorry."

♦

Sam's second visitor on Saturday was not expected. He stopped at a guard station by the front gate, and produced some identification. He explained that he was the brother of Sam Cayhall, and had been told he could visit Sam on death row any time before the planned execution date. The guard stepped inside and made a few phone calls.

The guard instructed the visitor to park his car, and within a few minutes a white prison van appeared. The visitor was driven to the front entrance of MSU, where he was searched by two guards. They led him into the empty visitors' room.

Sam was typing a letter when the guards stopped at his door. "Let's go, Sam. You have a visitor."

Sam stopped typing. "Who is it?"

"Your brother."

Sam put his typewriter on the shelf. "Which brother?"

When Sam stepped into the visitors' room, he looked at the

man sitting on the other side of the screen. It was a face he didn't recognize. Sam stared at the guards until they left the room and shut the door.

"Do I know you?" he asked finally.

"Yes," the man answered.

"From where?"

"From the past, Sam. From Greenville and Jackson and Vicksburg."

"Wedge?"

The man nodded slowly. Sam sank down in his chair. "God, I was hoping you were dead."

"Sorry. Here I am, Sam."

"I hate you more than any person has ever been hated. If I had a gun right now I'd blow you to hell and laugh until I cried. God, I hate you."

"Do you treat all your visitors like this, Sam?"

"What do you want, Wedge?"

"I won't keep you long. I just wanted to say that I'm here, and I'm watching things closely, and I'm very pleased that my name has not been mentioned. I certainly hope that this continues. I've been very effective at keeping people quiet. Just go on and take our little secret to your grave and no one gets hurt, OK?"

"Leave, Wedge. And don't ever come back."

"Sure. I hate to say it, Sam, but I hope they gas you."

♦

Sleep was becoming a battle. Adam's mind was burdened with the events of the past two weeks, and his mind raced wildly with what was coming. He slept little on Saturday night, and was awake for long periods. When he finally awoke for the last time, the sun was up. Lee had promised to make him breakfast, but as he pulled up his jeans and slipped on a T-shirt, he could not smell cooking.

The kitchen was quiet. He called Lee's name. Her bedroom door was open, so he quickly checked every room. She was not on the balcony. A sick feeling came over him and grew worse with each empty room.

◆

Sam had another unexpected guest on Sunday. He was a gray-haired man with a friendly face and a warm smile.

"Mr. Cayhall, my name is Ralph Griffin, and I'm the chaplain here at Parchman. I'm new, so we haven't met."

Sam nodded, and said, "Nice to meet you. I knew the previous chaplain. I didn't like him much."

"Yes, I've heard he wasn't very popular."

"That could be because he was in favor of the death penalty. Can you imagine? He was called by God to help us, but he believed we should die."

"Do you believe in God?"

"Yes, I do. Do you believe in the death penalty?"

"No, I don't."

Sam studied him for a while. "Are you serious?"

"Killing is wrong, Mr. Cayhall. If in fact you are guilty of your crime, then you were wrong to kill. It's also wrong for the government to kill you. Jesus didn't want us to kill as a punishment. He taught love and forgiveness."

"That's the way I read the Bible."

"I just wanted to introduce myself. I'd like to talk to you during the next few days. I'd like to pray with you if you want. You know the rules around here, don't you? During your last few hours you're allowed to have only two people present. Your lawyer and your spiritual adviser. I'll be honored to stay with you."

"Thanks. No one really wants to die, you know. Not even me."

"I've read about your grandson. That must be heartwarming. I know you're proud of him." Sam smiled and looked at the floor. "Anyway," Griffin continued, "I'll be around. Would you like me to come back tomorrow?"

"That would be nice."

◆

Every inmate of the Row was familiar with every step of an execution. Those who had been there a long time had lived through four executions over the past eight years.

The day before the execution, the inmate was taken from his cell for the last time and placed in the Observation Cell. It was the last cell in the row, and the nearest to the Isolation Room, which was next to the Chamber Room. He waited in Observation, his lawyer with him. A minister or spiritual adviser was also allowed in the cell. The Row was always dark and very quiet. Some of the inmates would hold hands and pray through the bars. Others would lie on their beds and wonder when their time would come.

At eleven, the guards would come and take the inmate to the Isolation Room. He would step into the hallway and there would be shouts of support from the other inmates, many of whom would be in tears. The Isolation Room was a small room, with nothing in it except a folding bed. The inmate would sit on the bed with his lawyer by his side.

Next door was the Chamber Room. It was approximately fifteen feet by twelve, with the gas chamber in the center of it. The executioner would be hard at work. Behind the chamber were three windows, covered for the moment by black curtains. On the other side of the windows was the witness room.

At five minutes before midnight, the inmate would be taken into the chamber. The Chamber Room was always filled with people, all anxious to help, all there to watch a man die. The guards would back him into the chamber, secure him, close the door, and kill him.

Sam's cell was eight doors from the Observation Cell, about forty-eight feet. Another twenty feet to the Isolation Room, then another twelve feet to the chamber. As Sam lay on his bed in his cell, he calculated again that he was approximately eighty-five feet from the gas chamber. He looked at his calendar. Only eight more days.

♦

Packer went to Sam's cell at five-thirty in the morning. Sam was waiting, and they left quietly. They walked through the kitchen, where breakfast was being prepared. Packer opened a door and gestured to Sam to follow quickly. They stepped outside, into the darkness. Sam looked at the square brick room to his right, the building that housed the gas chamber. Packer pulled his elbow, and they walked together to the east end of the row, where another guard was watching and waiting. The guard handed Sam a large cup of coffee, and led him through a gate into an exercise yard. It was fenced and wired, with two benches. Packer said he would return in an hour, and left with the guard.

Sam stood still for a long time, drinking the hot coffee and enjoying the landscape. He saw the guard in the tower sitting under a light and watching him. He slowly walked to a bench and sat down.

How thoughtful of these kind people to grant his request to see one final sunrise. He hadn't seen one in nine and a half years, and at first Nugent had said no. Then Packer explained to the colonel that it was OK, no security risk at all, and why not? The man was supposed to die in a few days. Packer would take responsibility for it.

Sam stared at the eastern sky, where a hint of orange was visible through scattered clouds. This would be his final sunrise, he truly believed that. Too many people wanted him dead. The gas chamber was not being used often enough. It was time for an execution, and he was next in line.

The sky grew brighter and the clouds began to disappear. Though he was forced to watch this wonderful act of nature through a chain-link fence, it was still satisfying. Just a few more days and the fences would be gone. The bars and wire and prison cells would be left for someone else.

Chapter 10   The Rabbit

The afternoon drive to Parchman was not a particularly pleasant one. Garner Goodman sat in the front seat as Adam drove. Adam had just heard from New Orleans and from the district court. He'd lost twice. The Fifth Circuit agreed with the decision of the federal court on the claim that the gas chamber was cruel, and the district court denied the claim that Benjamin Keyes had performed ineffectively at trial. Adam now had to perfect appeals on both claims, with Goodman's help.

In the back seat of the car sat the psychiatrist, Dr. Swinn, a cold, unsmiling man in a black suit. He had wild, bushy hair, dark eyes hidden behind thick glasses, and was completely incapable of making conversation. He did not utter a single word on the journey from Memphis to Parchman.

The examination had been arranged to take place in the prison hospital, and Dr. Swinn had informed Adam that neither he nor Goodman could be present during his examination of Sam. A prison van met them at the front gate, and carried Dr. Swinn to the hospital. Adam and Goodman sat and drank iced tea in the restaurant which served food to the office workers and prison employees.

After a time Adam excused himself and found a pay phone in the corner. Lee did not answer the phone.

♦

Back in the Memphis office, Darlene typed Dr. Swinn's report on Sam while Adam and Garner Goodman worked on the legal case to accompany it. The report was twenty pages long in its first version. Swinn was a man who'd sell an opinion to the highest bidder, and Adam hated him and people like him. He traveled the country giving evidence, able to say this today and that tomorrow, depending on who had the deepest pockets. But for the moment, he was working for them, and he was good. Sam was suffering from advanced mental breakdown. He had reached a point where he did not know the nature of his punishment. He lacked the necessary understanding to be executed, and therefore the execution would not serve any purpose. It was not an entirely unique legal argument, and the courts had not exactly accepted it with enthusiasm in the past. But, thought Adam, what was there to lose? Goodman seemed to be more than a little optimistic, particularly because of Sam's age. He could not remember an execution of a man over the age of fifty.

They, Darlene included, worked until almost eleven.

♦

Garner Goodman did not return to Chicago on Wednesday morning, but instead flew to Jackson, Mississippi. He rented a car at the airport and drove straight to the state courthouse. Four years earlier, during the days and hours prior to the Maynard Tole execution, Goodman had made this same journey on two occasions. There was a different governor then, a different client, and a different crime. Tole had murdered several people in two days of violent crime, and it had been difficult to find any pity for him. He hoped Sam Cayhall was different. His crime was ancient history to many Mississippians.

The governor's office was on the second floor. Goodman handed his card to the lovely receptionist. He had made an appointment to see the governor at one o'clock, but that time came and went without comment. The receptionist apologized at two. At 2.15, he was told the governor could see him.

McAllister was standing by the window with his jacket off. "Hello, Mr. Goodman," he said, with a hand held out toward him and teeth flashing brilliantly.

"Governor, my pleasure," Goodman said. "Thanks for seeing me."

They sat at the conference table. "I understand there've been quite a lot of claims and appeals in the past few days," McAllister said.

"Yes, sir. As you know, all Sam's major claims have been made and decided on over the past few years. What you see now are the desperate appeals, but they often work. I'd say fifty-fifty, today, seven days away."

McAllister thought about it for a few seconds. "I'm a little confused, Mr. Goodman. Your client does not know we're meeting. He's opposed to the idea of a clemency hearing. So why are we here?"

"People change. I've been here before. I've watched men count down their last days. It does strange things to the mind. As a lawyer, I have to explore every possibility."

"Are you asking for a hearing?"

"Yes, sir. A closed hearing. In two days' time, maybe."

"Why do you want the hearing closed?"

"It's really best for everyone not to have the publicity. It's less pressure on you, Governor, and we, frankly, don't want the public to see Ruth Kramer talking about her little boys." The real reason was something else altogether. Adam was sure that the only way to talk Sam into a clemency hearing was to promise him it would not be a public show.

"I guess that makes sense," the governor said. "However, there's no real reason for such a hearing unless you have something new to add. I know this case, Mr. Goodman. I smelled the smoke. I saw the bodies. I cannot change my mind unless there's something new."

"Such as?"

"Such as a name. You give me the name of Sam's partner in this crime, and I'll agree to a hearing. Otherwise this is a waste of time."

"I've always thought there must have been someone else behind the bombing. But why is it so important?"

"It is important because I make the final decision, Mr. Goodman. If Sam deserves the death penalty, then I have no problem watching while it happens. But if he doesn't, then the execution should be stopped. I'm a young man. I do not want to carry the guilt of a wrong decision for the rest of my life."

"Very well, we'll talk to Sam again. I'll let you know if we get anywhere. We are requesting a hearing as soon as possible, in any case."

"The request is denied unless Sam talks."

♦

Colonel Nugent sat at the end of a long table in the front of a room filled with guards and other staff. Nugent looked at his watch, then began his little talk.

"We have six full days to prepare for the execution of Sam Cayhall. I am determined that this will take place smoothly, without problems.

"The inmate has at least three claims and appeals currently working their way through the various courts, and of course, anything might happen. We are in constant contact with the Attorney General's office. A delay could be granted at any moment, but that looks doubtful. The inmate is also expected to request a clemency hearing, but, frankly, that is not expected to be successful. From now until next Wednesday, we will be prepared."

Nugent's words were strong and clear. He had center-stage and was obviously enjoying every moment of it. He looked at his notes, and continued. "The gas chamber itself is being prepared. It's old and it hasn't been used in two years, so we're being very careful. We'll do a complete practice over the weekend. I have collected a list of volunteers for the execution team.

"Now, we've received a lot of requests from the media for all sorts of things. They want to interview everyone. They want to witness the execution. They want pictures of his cell and the chamber. Typical media silliness, but we must deal with it. There will be no contact with any member of the press unless I first approve it. That applies to every single employee of this prison.

"We're also expecting trouble from outside. About ten minutes ago, the first group of Ku Klux Klansmen arrived at the front gate. We've also heard that other such groups will be here shortly, and it appears that they plan to protest until this thing is over. We'll watch them closely. It is likely that groups of death penalty supporters will come and cause trouble. We plan to keep these two groups separated, for obvious reasons."

Nugent stood up stiffly at the end of the table. "This case will attract a lot of attention, a lot of media. We must act professionally at all times."

◆

Between the western edge of Highway 49 and the front of the administrative buildings at Parchman, a distance of 50 yards, there was a grassy piece of land. It was where the death penalty protestors set up camp at every execution.

When Adam arrived Friday morning, he counted seven Ku Klux Klansmen in white clothing. They had plenty of supplies with them. These guys were planning to stay. Adam stared at them as he rolled to a stop at the front gate. He began walking slowly in their direction. Their signs demanded freedom for Sam Cayhall, a political prisoner. Gas the real criminals, but release Sam. For some reason, Adam was not comforted by their demands.

"What do you want?" demanded one of them. "Who the hell are you?"

The others stopped what they were doing and stared.

"I'm Sam's grandson."

"Then you're on our side," one said, with relief.

"No. I'm not one of you."

"That's right. He's with that firm of Chicago Jews."

"Why are you people here?" Adam asked.

"We're trying to save Sam. Looks like you're not going to do it."

"He wouldn't be here if it wasn't for the Klan."

They stood there, uncertain what to do next. He was, after all, the grandson of Sam Cayhall, their champion.

"Why don't you leave?" Adam asked. "Sam doesn't want you here."

"Why don't you go to hell?" the youngest one suggested. "We're not leavin'. We'll be here till the end. We plan to make a lot of noise."

"Great. That'll get your pictures in the papers. That's what this is all about, isn't it?"

Car doors shut loudly somewhere behind Adam, and a television crew got out of a van and came toward them. Adam walked toward his car without stopping.

◆

Sam was amused when Adam told him about the Klansmen.

"I told them to leave," Adam said. "Just a few minutes ago. I exchanged words with them. They don't care about you, Sam, they're just using this execution for publicity. They want you dead, Sam. It's great advertising for them."

"You really told them that?" Sam asked, smiling, and with a trace of pride.

"Yeah. Sam, we need to talk about your claims. The Mississippi Supreme Court just turned down our claim that you are mentally unfit. The US Supreme Court denied the cruelty appeal. Fifth Circuit isn't responding to the ineffectiveness claim. Not a very good morning."

"The Jackson TV station this morning said I've requested a clemency hearing from the governor," Sam said. "That can't be true. I didn't approve it."

"Relax, Sam. It's routine."

"It certainly is not. I thought we had an agreement. They even had McAllister on, talking about it. I warned you."

"McAllister is the least of our problems, Sam. The request was a formality. We don't have to take part."

Sam shook his head with a frown. Adam watched him closely. He wasn't really angry.

Sam suddenly jumped to his feet and walked across the office and back. He finally stopped. "I want you to do me a favor," he said, quietly. He breathed slowly.

"I'm listening," Adam said.

Sam picked up an envelope. He handed it to Adam.

"I want you to deliver that."

"To whom?"

"Quince Lincoln. I've worked on it for a week," he said, "but I've thought about it for forty years."

"What's in the letter?" Adam asked slowly.

"An apology. Joe Lincoln was a good man. I killed him for no reason. I've always felt bad about it. Really bad. There's nothing I can do now except say I'm sorry."

"I'd be happy to do it. If I can find Quince."

"Wait until I'm dead. You'll have plenty of time then."

Sam picked up two more envelopes. The name of Ruth Kramer was typed on one, and Elliott Kramer on the other. "Those are for the Kramers. Deliver them, but wait until the execution is over. I don't want them to think I'm doing this because I want their pity in my dying hours."

"You're sure you're going to die, aren't you, Sam?"

"It doesn't look good. I'm getting prepared, just in case. I've hurt a lot of people, Adam. When you're going to die, you think about the damage you've done."

Sam placed the Kramers' letters next to Quince's. Three letters, three dead bodies. How many more letters would Sam produce? How many more victims were out there?

◆

The rabbit had been trapped in the woods at Parchman by two of the guards, who named him Sam for the occasion. He was the largest of the four brown rabbits captured. The other three had already been eaten.

Late at night, Sam the rabbit and his handlers, with Colonel Nugent and the execution team, parked by the Maximum Security Unit in prison vans. The execution team went into the Chamber Room. The room was spotless and newly painted. Nugent had organized that. Now he walked around, inspecting everything – pointing and nodding and frowning. At last he seemed satisfied.

"Get the rabbit," Nugent ordered. One of the handlers brought the animal in. He sat innocently in a wire cage which was handed to the guards. They carefully placed the cage in the chair, then began their task of tying in an imaginary man. Wrists, knees, ankles, head, and the rabbit was ready for the gas. The guards left the chamber.

The door was shut tight, and Nugent signaled for the executioner, who placed a container of acid into the tube which ran into the bottom of the chamber. He pulled a lever, and the container made its way to the bowl under the chair. Nugent stepped to one of the windows and watched carefully. The other members of the team did the same.

The poisonous gas was released slowly and rose up. At first, the rabbit didn't react to the steam, then it hit him. He stiffened, jumped a few times, then started shaking violently. In less than a minute, he was dead.

Nugent smiled as he looked at his watch. "Clear it," he ordered, and the gas was released into the air outside through an opening in the top of the chamber. Most of the execution team went outside. It would be at least fifteen minutes before the chamber could be opened and the rabbit removed. Then they had to wash it all down. Nugent was still inside, so they smoked and laughed together.

Less than sixty feet away, the windows above the cells were open. Sam could hear their voices. A death row inmate hears everything, and soon learns what every sound means. He can certainly hear the opening and closing of the door to the Chamber Room. He can hear the satisfied laughter of the execution team.

Sam leaned on his elbows and watched the windows above the hallway. They were practicing for him out there.

Chapter 11   Confessions

Though he'd worn the white clothing of the Klan as a much younger man, Donnie Cayhall kept his distance from the lines of

75

Klansmen near the front gate at Parchman. Security was tight; armed guards watched the protestors. Many of the Klan members held signs demanding freedom for Sam Cayhall.

Donnie reported to the security guard. His name was checked, and a few minutes later a van came for him. His brother had been at Parchman for nine and a half years, and every month Donnie had sent Sam a box of cigarettes and some cash. He had tried to visit at least once a year, but he was ashamed to admit that the last visit was two years ago.

Donnie Cayhall was sixty-one, the youngest of the four Cayhall brothers. All had followed the teachings of their father and joined the Klan in their teenage years. Later Donnie had traveled the world, and he had lost interest in the Klan.

He was searched, and shown to the front office, just inside the entrance to the Row. As the big day approached, prisoners were allowed to meet their visitors there, without a time limit.

Sam was brought in a few minutes later, and the two men were left alone. Donnie put his arms around his brother tightly for a long time, and when he let go both men had tears in their eyes. They were of similar height and build, though Sam looked twenty years older. He sat on the desk, and Donnie sat near him.

"Any good news?" Donnie asked, certain of the answer.

"No. None. The courts are turning everything down. They're going to do it, Donnie. They're going to kill me. They'll put me in the chamber and gas me like an animal."

Donnie's face showed his disappointment. "I'm sorry, Sam."

"I'm sorry, too, but I'll be glad when it's done."

"Don't say that."

"I mean it. I'm an old man. I'm tired of living in a cage."

"Can't your lawyer do something?"

"He's trying everything, but it looks hopeless. I want you to meet him."

"I saw his picture in the paper. He doesn't look like a Cayhall. Smart kid?"

"Yeah, he's great. He's staying with Lee in Memphis," Sam said with pride. Because of him, his daughter and his grandson had become close. "I need something from you, Donnie. And it'll cost a little money."

"Sure. Anything."

Sam pulled at the waist of his red jumpsuit. "These're called reds, and I've worn them every day for almost ten years. This is what the State of Mississippi expects me to wear when it kills me. But I have a right to wear anything I want. It would mean a lot if I could die in some nice clothes."

Donnie was suddenly overcome by emotion. He tried to speak, but words didn't come. He nodded, and managed to say, "Sure, Sam."

"A pair of those work pants would be nice – you know, the ones I wore for years. A white shirt of some sort, one with buttons. A pair of white socks, and some kind of cheap shoes. Nothing expensive. Hell, I'll just wear them once, won't I? Do you mind?"

"No, Sam. I'll do it today."

◆

Sunday was a day of unexpected peace and quiet for Adam. There wasn't a lot to do this day, Day Three before the execution. It was unlikely that any court would make a decision on a Sunday. The Fifth Circuit wasn't responding to the ineffectiveness claim. The district court had the mental claim. Tomorrow would be crazy. And Tuesday would be terrible.

Adam was alone at Lee's place. Lee was still missing. Adam had called at Auburn House, but no one there had seen her for several days. He had spoken to Lee's husband, Phelps, who did not know where she was.

There was unfinished business in Lee's bedroom, a matter Adam had tried to forget but couldn't. For days now he had thought of the book in her drawer, the book with a photo of a young black man hanging by a rope, and somewhere under his feet a crowd of proud white people. Adam had put the picture together in his mind, adding faces, drawing the tree, the rope. He had imagined the picture for days now, and it was time to finally take a look.

Adam went to the front door and looked out over the parking lot, just to make sure Lee hadn't decided to return. He actually locked the door to her bedroom, and pulled open the drawers.

The book was in the third drawer, lying on top of some clothes. It was thick and covered in green fabric – *Southern Negroes in Hard Times*, published in 1947. Adam took it and sat on the edge of the bed. There were two lynching photos in the center of the book. The first showed a horrible scene with two Klansmen holding guns. A badly beaten black man swung from a rope behind them, his eyes half open, his face bloody and broken. *KKK lynching, Central Mississippi, 1939*, explained the words under the picture.

Adam sucked in his breath with horror, then turned to the second picture. This was not quite so horrible. A lifeless body at the end of a rope could be seen only from the chest down. The man's shirt was torn, probably by a whip, but no blood was visible. The black man was very thin, his oversized pants pulled in tightly at the waist. He was barefoot. The rope that held his body was tied to a lower branch in the background. A group had gathered to celebrate just inches under the hanging feet. It was a real party. Adam counted seventeen people in the group – men, women, and boys. Every single one was staring at the camera without shame or worry, without the slightest hint that a wrong had been committed. *Lynching in rural Mississippi, 1936*, he read.

Adam looked at these people and wondered how many of them were Cayhalls. Sam was in the front row, resting on one knee between two other young men. He was fifteen or sixteen. Adam studied the clear, beautiful eyes of his grandfather, and his heart ached. He was just a boy, born into a household where hatred of blacks and others was simply a way of life. How much of it could be blamed on him? This was the only world he ever knew.

♦

Sam placed the Sunday newspaper on the desk and inspected his visitor. The chaplain wore faded jeans and a black shirt with a white minister's collar.

"Have you been praying, Sam?" Ralph Griffin asked, as he pulled a chair very near the desk and sat in it.

"Not really. What's the hurry? I guess you and I'll be doing lots of praying on Tuesday night."

"If you want. I'll be here."

"I want you to be with me up to the last moment, if you don't mind. You and my lawyer."

"What exactly do you want to pray about, Sam?"

"Well, I'd like to know that when I leave this world, all the bad things I've done have been forgiven."

"God expects us to confess our sins to him and ask for forgiveness."

"All of them? One at a time?"

"Yes, the ones we can remember."

"Then we'd better start now. It'll take some time. I want to say a good prayer for the Kramers. And also the Lincolns."

"Who are the Lincolns?"

"It's a long story. More victims. There was Joe Lincoln, but I've already written a letter to his family and told them I was sorry. I always felt bad about killing him."

Sam stopped and leaned on the wall. He looked at the floor as he spoke. "And there were two white men who killed my father at a funeral, many years ago. They served some time in jail, and when they got out, me and my brothers killed both of them, but I never felt bad about it. They were real bad guys, and they'd killed our father."

"Killing is always wrong, Sam."

"I know that now. Life has a new meaning when you're on death row." Sam walked the length of the room. The chaplain waited.

"There were a couple of lynchings, years ago," Sam said, unable to look Griffin in the eyes.

"Two?"

"I think. Maybe three. No, yes, there were three, but at the first one I was just a kid, a small boy, and all I did was watch from the bushes. So that doesn't count, does it?"

"No."

Sam's shoulders sank against the wall. He closed his eyes. "The second one was a crowd of us. I was about fifteen, I guess, and I was right in the middle of it. A girl had got pregnant by an African boy. She said he forced her to have sex. There was some doubt about that. Anyway, we got the boy, took him out, and lynched him. I was as guilty as the rest of them."

"God will forgive you, Sam."

"Are you sure?"

"I'm positive. If you sincerely ask forgiveness. What about the other lynching?"

Sam began shaking his head, backward and forward, eyes closed. "Now, I can't begin to talk about that one. I don't know if I can talk to anybody about it. Even God."

"Sure you can. Just close your eyes one night, while you're in your cell, and confess all those deeds to God. He'll forgive you."

Sam walked to the desk and sat on the corner next to Griffin. "You stay close, OK? There's some bad things buried in my soul. I'll need some help to get them out."

◆

The front office was filled with blue smoke when Adam entered. Sam was alone again, smoking at the desk and reading about himself in the Sunday paper.

"Tell me you've brought some good news," said Sam.

Adam shook his head and sat down. "No. Nothing's changed. The courts aren't working this weekend."

Sam picked up some envelopes and handed them to Adam. "More deliveries for me?" he asked.

"Yeah, but they can wait until it's over."

"To whom?"

"One is to the Pinder family I bombed in Vicksburg. One is to the Jewish church I bombed in Jackson. One is to the Jewish property agent in Jackson. There may be others."

"What do these letters say?"

"What do you think they say?"

"I don't know. That you're sorry, I guess."

"Smart boy. I apologize and ask them to forgive me." He reached for another cigarette. "What's happened to Lee?"

"Do you want to see her?"

"I think so. Can she come?"

"It may be difficult, but I'll try. She's not at home at the moment. She's gone to a place where they can help her with her drinking," Adam lied. He was still hoping that Lee would be found before Tuesday.

"She's an alcoholic?"

"Yes. She told me she's had a problem for many years. It's nothing new."

81

"My children didn't have a chance, did they?"

"What's this?" Adam asked, pointing to another envelope.

Sam handed it to him. "I want you to take this to the front gate, and I want you to find the leader of those Klansmen, and I want you to read it to him. Tell the cameras to film it, so people know what it says."

"What *does* it say?"

"I ask them all to go home. To leave me alone, so that I can die in peace. It tells them that I am no longer a member of the Ku Klux Klan."

"I'm not so sure it's a good idea right now, Sam."

"Why not?"

"Because as we speak, we're telling the Fifth Circuit that you're basically a vegetable, incapable of putting together thoughts like these."

Sam was suddenly angry. "You lawyers," he shouted. "Don't you ever give up? It's finished, Adam, stop playing games."

"It's not finished."

"I just want it all to end." Sam threw away his cigarette and held Adam's shoulders. "Look at me, son. I'm an old man. I can't stand this waiting. Please allow me to die quietly."

His hands were shaking. His breathing was difficult. Adam searched his bright blue eyes, and saw a single tear run slowly down his cheek.

"I don't want you to die, Sam."

Sam squeezed his shoulders harder. "Why not?" he demanded.

"Because I've just found you. You're my grandfather."

Sam released Adam and took a step back. "I'm sorry you found me like this. I'm sorry I'm not a better grandfather. Look at me," he said, looking down at his legs, "a sad wreck of a man in a red monkey suit. And look at you. A fine young man with a beautiful education and a bright future. Why am I here? We have the same blood. I've spent my life hating people. You don't hate anybody. Where did I go wrong?"

Chapter 12   In Court

Monday, August 6, 6 a.m. Forty-two more hours. Adam had slept less than three hours. He entered his office and locked the door.

He waited until seven, then called Slattery's office in Jackson. There was no answer. Slattery was doing nothing about the mental incompetence claim.

The phone rang. The clerk at the Fifth Circuit informed him that the court was denying Sam's claim of ineffective representation. The claim should have been made years ago, and it was now too late to consider it. Adam put the phone down, and went to find coffee. Darlene arrived, tired, at seven-thirty. Adam asked her to send the ineffectiveness claim on to the US Supreme Court.

Adam's head was aching as he packed most of the Cayhall file in a large briefcase and a box. He gave Darlene a list of instructions. Then he left the office, the Memphis branch of Kravitz and Bane, and never returned.

◆

In the federal courthouse in Jackson, Breck Jefferson entered the office of his boss, Judge F. Flynn Slattery, who was talking angrily on the phone. Breck held a legal pad filled with notes.

"Yes?" Slattery asked crossly, banging down the phone.

"We need to talk about Cayhall," Breck said seriously. "You know we've got his claim of mental incompetence."

"Let's deny it and get rid of it. I'm too busy to worry with it.

Let Cayhall take it to the Fifth Circuit. I don't want it lying around here."

Breck looked troubled, and his words came slower. "But there's something you need to take a look at."

"Surely not, Breck. What is it?"

"He may have a genuine claim."

Slattery's face fell. "Are you joking? What is it? We have a trial starting in thirty minutes. There's a jury waiting out there."

Breck Jefferson had been the number 2 student in his law class, and Slattery trusted him completely. "They're claiming Sam Cayhall does not have the mental competence to face an execution. They have an expert who's willing to give evidence. We can't ignore it."

"I don't believe this."

"You'd better look at it."

His Honor frowned. "Sit down. Let me see it."

◆

Adam went to the phone and pressed the numbers. He had a message to ring Garner Goodman in Jackson. Urgently.

"Garner, it's Adam. What's happening?"

"Get yourself down here now," Goodman said calmly. "Things are moving."

"Why? What is it?"

"Looks like one of your claims is being taken seriously."

"Which one?"

"Mental incompetence. Slattery wants a hearing at five this afternoon. I've already talked to Dr. Swinn, and he's ready. He'll land in Jackson at three-thirty and be ready to give evidence."

"I'm on my way," Adam said.

"Meet me at the governor's office."

◆

By noon, Judge Slattery was fully in charge of the situation, and though he tried hard to hide it, he was enjoying immensely this brief interval in the center of the storm. First, he had dismissed the jury and lawyers in today's civil trial. He had spoken to the clerk of the Fifth Circuit in New Orleans, then to Justice McNeely, then to Supreme Court Justice Edward F. Allbright in Washington. Allbright was following every stage of the case. The reporters quickly learned that a hearing of some type was going to happen, and the phones in Slattery's office began to ring.

Breck Jefferson read through countless law books and scattered his notes over the long conference table. Slattery talked to the governor, the Attorney General, Garner Goodman, dozens of others. He walked around his massive desk, holding the phone, enjoying all the madness.

◆

Adam parked in the grounds of the state buildings. Goodman was waiting under a tree with his jacket off and sleeves rolled up, his bow tie perfect.

"The governor wants to see you at two."

"What's on the governor's mind?" Adam asked.

"Who knows? He wants to meet with you privately. Maybe he's planning some publicity trick for the media. Maybe he's sincere."

◆

The governor and the young lawyer were alone in the vast office. McAllister's words were calm, almost tired. "It's strange, you know – you're the grandson, and you've known him for less than a month. But I've known him for years. And I've always thought that I'd look forward to this day. I've wanted him to die, you know, to be punished for killing the boys." His words sounded genuine, as if two old friends were exchanging gossip. "But now I'm not so sure. Adam, the pressure's affecting me."

He was either being very honest, or he was a talented actor. Adam couldn't tell.

"Has Sam told you anything new about the bombing?" McAllister asked.

"I can't reveal what Sam's told me. But no, he hasn't."

"Maybe he acted alone, I don't know."

"What difference would it make today, the day before the execution?"

"If I knew that someone else was responsible for the bombs, for the killings, then I could not allow his execution. I could stop it, you know."

"You believe he had help. The FBI agent in charge of the investigation believes it too. Why don't you just act on your beliefs and grant clemency?"

"Because we're not certain."

"So, you just need one word, one name from Sam. It won't happen, Governor. I've tried."

"Who's he protecting?"

"I've no idea."

"Is Sam really insane?"

"Our expert says he is. We'll do our best to persuade Judge Slattery."

"I know, but really? You've spent hours with him. Does he know what's happening?"

Adam decided against honesty. McAllister was not a friend, and could not be trusted. "He's pretty sad," Adam admitted. "Frankly, I'm surprised any person can keep his mind after a few months on death row. Sam was an old man when he got there, and he's slowly faded."

Adam couldn't tell if the governor believed this, but he was listening. "I gave you my private number, Adam. Let's keep in touch tomorrow."

◆

The main courtroom in the federal building was full. Adam sat with Garner Goodman. The Attorney General, Roxburgh, sat at the state's table with half a dozen assistants. Two rows behind them sat the governor. The rest of the crowd was mainly reporters – no cameras were allowed. There were some law students, other lawyers, and members of the public. In the back row sat Rollie Wedge.

Everyone stood as Slattery made his entrance. "Be seated," he said into his microphone. He explained the purpose of the hearing. He was not in the mood for long arguments and pointless questions, he told the lawyers.

"Is Mr. Hall ready?" he asked.

Adam stood nervously. "Yes, sir. I call Dr. Anson Swinn."

Swinn went to the witness stand. Adam stood at the table in the center of the courtroom, holding his notes and pushing himself to be strong. He began by asking Swinn some basic questions about his education and training. With his black hair, black beard, black glasses, and black suit, he indeed gave the appearance of a great expert.

In response to Adam's questions, Swinn talked about his two hours with Sam Cayhall on the previous Tuesday. He described his physical condition, and made Sam appear a very sick man. He was quite probably insane. He had difficulty answering even basic questions like, "What did you eat for breakfast? Who is in the cell next to you? When did your wife die?" And on and on.

In Swinn's opinion, Sam Cayhall did not appreciate the fact that he was about to die, did not understand why he was being executed, and certainly didn't realize he was being punished for a crime. Mr. Cayhall's case was one of the worst he'd seen.

Under different circumstances, Adam would have been horrified to use a witness so obviously full of exaggeration and untruths. But now he was proud of this strange little man – a human life could be saved.

Swinn talked about the causes of Sam's problems. He described the horrors of living in a cell, near the gas chamber, twenty-three hours a day; of being denied companionship, good food, sex, movement, exercise, fresh air. He'd worked with many death row inmates and knew their problems well. Sam, of course, was very different because of his age. The average death row inmate was thirty-one years old, but Sam was sixty when he first arrived at Parchman. Physically and mentally, he was not suited for it.

When Adam had finished his questions, it was the Attorney General's turn. He began by asking about the large fee Swinn was charging for his services. Slattery was not impressed by this argument; he knew that all experts get paid for giving evidence. Roxburgh tried to question Swinn's professional qualifications, but without success; the man was a well-educated, well-trained, experienced psychiatrist. The Attorney General then began a long series of questions about other cases in which Swinn had given evidence.

"Where are you going with this?" Slattery interrupted.

"Your Honor, we are attempting to show that the witness is prepared to state some wild opinions if the money is right."

"Lawyers do that every day, Mr. Roxburgh." There was some laughter in the audience. "I don't want to hear it," Slattery said sharply. "Now move on."

Roxburgh asked some questions about Swinn's examination of Sam, and Swinn answered each question well, repeating much of the sad description of Sam Cayhall. Roxburgh scored no points, and returned to his seat.

The next witness Adam called was a surprise. It was E. Garner

Goodman. Goodman first gave a brief history of his firm's representation of Sam Cayhall.

"Does Kravitz and Bane represent Mr. Cayhall at this moment?" Adam asked.

"Indeed we do."

"And you're here in Jackson at this moment working on the case?"

"That's correct."

"Mr. Goodman, do you believe Sam Cayhall has told his lawyers everything about the Kramer bombing?"

"No, I do not."

Rollie Wedge sat up and listened carefully.

"Would you please explain?"

"Certainly. I have always suspected that another person was with Sam Cayhall during the Kramer bombing, and the bombings which came before it. Mr. Cayhall has always refused to discuss this with me, his lawyer, and even now will not cooperate with his attorneys. There are facts that, at this point in the case, we should know – but he won't tell us."

Wedge was both nervous and relieved. Sam was not talking, but his lawyers were trying everything.

Roxburgh had little to ask Goodman, and he returned to his seat.

"Call your first witness, Mr. Roxburgh," Slattery said.

"The state calls Colonel George Nugent," Roxburgh announced. Nugent came to the witness stand. His clothes were newly ironed. His boots were shining.

"When did you last see Sam Cayhall?" Roxburgh asked.

"This morning. We moved him to the Observation Cell."

"Was he mentally active?"

"He was extremely active and aware. He asked why he was being moved. He understood what was happening."

"Did you see him yesterday?"

"Yes."

"And was he able to speak, or just lying around like a vegetable?"

"We talked about his last meal, his witnesses, what to do with his personal possessions. Things like that."

"Is he aware he is going to be executed?"

Nugent burst into laughter. "Of course. He knows perfectly well what's going on. He's not crazy."

Roxburgh asked about prior meetings with Sam, and Nugent spared no details. He seemed to remember every word Sam had uttered in the past two weeks, especially his nasty and threatening remarks.

Adam knew it was all true. He and Goodman decided not to ask Nugent any questions. Little could be gained from it.

Roxburgh's next witness was Sergeant Clyde Packer. Adam was not surprised at the effect of Packer's evidence. He was an honest man who simply told what he'd seen. He'd known Sam for nine and a half years, and the prisoner was the same today as when he'd first arrived. He typed letters and law papers all day long, read many books, especially legal ones. In Packer's humble opinion, Sam was as mentally active now as he'd been nine and a half years ago. And his mind was very quick.

Perhaps the turning point of the hearing came when Packer told the story of Sam wanting to see a sunrise before he died. Sam had quietly made the request. He knew he was going to die, said he was ready to go, and that he'd like to go out early one morning and see the sun come up. So Packer arranged it and Sam spent an hour drinking coffee and waiting for the sun. Afterward, he was very grateful.

Adam had no questions for Packer.

Roxburgh announced that the next witness was Ralph Griffin, the prison chaplain.

"Do you know Sam Cayhall?" Roxburgh asked him.

"I do."

"When did you last see him?"

"Yesterday."

"And how would you describe his mental condition?"

"I can't."

"I beg your pardon?"

"I can't describe his mental condition, because right now I'm his minister, and anything he says in my presence is strictly confidential. I can't give evidence against him."

Roxburgh paused, trying to decide what to do next. It was obvious he had not given any thought to this situation. Slattery settled the matter.

"A very good point. Mr. Roxburgh, this witness should not be here. Who's next?"

"No further witnesses," the Attorney General said.

His Honor looked at the crowded courtroom. "I will consider this matter and give an opinion, probably early in the morning. As soon as my decision is ready, we will inform the attorneys. You may all leave."

◆

Sam lay in the darkness and waited for midnight. He'd watched the late news and learned that the hearing had ended. His life was in the hands of a federal judge. He had twenty-four hours to live.

Chapter 13   The Chamber

Adam was in his car driving back to Parchman when he heard the news. The radio talk show host was filled with excitement as he discussed the latest developments in the Cayhall case. United States

91

District Court Judge F. Flynn Slattery had just denied Cayhall's claim to be mentally incompetent. An appeal would go to the Fifth Circuit within the hour. Sam Cayhall had just taken a huge step toward the Mississippi gas chamber, the host said dramatically.

As Adam cursed Slattery, his heart ached for Sam. He had failed as a lawyer. Sam had told him from the beginning that Mississippi wanted an execution. Other states, such as Louisiana and Texas and Florida, were killing at a better rate. It was time for Mississippi to execute someone. Adam finally believed him.

♦

Sam heard the news sitting on his bed in the Observation Cell. He stared at the television, watched the scenes switch from Jackson to Parchman and back again.

He pulled off his red jumpsuit for the last time, bundled it up and threw it in a corner. He neatly arranged his new clothes on the bed, then slowly unbuttoned the short-sleeved shirt and put it on. It fitted nicely. He slid his legs into the stiff work pants, pulled the zipper up and buttoned the waist. The pants were a little too long, so he sat on the bed and turned them up neatly. The cotton socks were comfortable. The shoes were a bit large but not a bad fit.

The sensation of being fully dressed in real clothes brought sudden, painful memories of the free world. These were the pants he'd worn for forty years, until he'd gone to prison. He wore them to work and he wore them to town. He wore them on fishing trips with Eddie, and he wore them at home with little Lee. It had been nine years and six months since he had worn these pants. Appropriate, he guessed, that he should now wear them to the gas chamber.

They'd be cut from his body, placed in a bag, and burned.

♦

Sam was in the front office when Adam arrived, sitting on the desk, admiring his shoes. Adam stepped close and inspected the clothing from shoes to shirt. Sam was smiling.

"You look nice, Sam," Adam said. "Really nice. Did Donnie bring these?"

"Yeah. They're just cheap ones. I started to order some designer clothes from New York, but I changed my mind – it's only an execution. It was a good feeling to take off that red prison suit. Any news for me?"

Adam looked serious. "Fifth Circuit just denied our appeal. We're on our way to the Supreme Court."

◆

Donnie Cayhall arrived for his last visit a few minutes before six. He was led straight to the front office, where he found his well-dressed brother laughing with Adam Hall. Sam introduced the two.

Donnie was clean and neat and sensibly dressed. He looked very like Sam, now that Sam had shaved and cut his hair. Donnie was genuinely happy to meet Adam and proud of the fact that he was a lawyer. He was a pleasant man with an easy smile, good teeth, but very sad eyes. "What's it look like?" he asked Adam.

"It's all in the Supreme Court."

"So there's still hope?"

"A little."

There was a pause. Donnie began to talk about their relatives, and Sam remembered a joke they had played many years ago on their old Aunt Finnie. The stories and the laughter grew. Adam smiled at the sight of these two old men laughing like boys.

At seven-thirty Sam's last meal arrived. He wasn't hungry, so it was a good thing he had only ordered ice-cream and coffee. He couldn't understand how some men expected to eat seven-course dinners before their execution.

The others watched Sam eating. At last Donnie got up. "I'd better go now, Sam. They'll be here in a minute."

The two men put their arms around each other and held each other for a long time. "I'm sorry, Sam," Donnie said, his voice shaking. "I'm so sorry."

They pulled apart, still holding each other's shoulders. "You take care," Sam said. "And thanks. You know, you're the only one who cared." Donnie bit his lip and hid his eyes from Sam. He shook hands with Adam, but could not utter a word as he left.

Sam sat on the desk, his feet swinging beneath him. "I really want this to end, Adam," he said. "This is cruel."

Adam could think of nothing to say.

Moments later, Nugent entered the room loudly. "Sam, it's time to go back to the Observation Cell," he said.

◆

The state executioner, a short, strong man named Bill Monday, was busy and very much in control. He would earn 500 dollars for his services if an execution took place. He was in a tiny closet known as the chemical room, less than five feet from the gas chamber, studying a checklist.

Nugent spoke to Monday; all was proceeding as planned. The room and the chair were being checked. The door was open to the outside, where an ambulance was already parked. There was an execution list, a chart of the twenty-nine steps to be taken to begin and complete the task. Nugent knew every step on the list.

◆

David McAllister was going to get a lot of attention. He changed into a dark navy suit, a fresh white shirt, and a dark tie. He combed and smoothed his hair and brushed his teeth, then checked both tie and teeth in a mirror. When he opened the door, two bodyguards were waiting for him. They walked with him to the area where a crowd of reporters and cameras pressed forward to hear his announcement. McAllister stood under the bright lights, a dozen microphones in front of him. It was a great moment. He waited for quiet, then spoke.

"The Supreme Court of the United States has just denied the last appeals from Sam Cayhall," he said dramatically. "And so, after all this time, justice has finally arrived for Sam Cayhall. His crime was committed twenty-three years ago. I have been asked by many people to pardon Mr. Cayhall, but I cannot do so. I cannot go against the judgment of our finest courts. Furthermore, I am not willing to go against the wishes of my friends, the Kramers." Another pause. "It is my greatest wish that the execution of Sam Cayhall will help remove a painful chapter in our state's sad history. May God have mercy on his soul."

The governor went out by a side door to a waiting car. A mile away, a helicopter was also waiting.

◆

As he walked, Adam wondered how many lawyers before him had made this short journey from the front office to the Observation Cell to inform a dying man that his last hopes were now gone.

Sam and the chaplain were sitting low on the bed, heads nearly touching in the darkness, whispering. They looked up at Adam, who sat next to Sam and placed his arm around his shoulders.

"The Supreme Court just denied everything," he said very softly. "And the governor just denied clemency."

Sam sank lower on the bed.

"Lord have mercy," Ralph Griffin said.

"Then it's all finished," Sam said.

"There's nothing left," Adam whispered.

There was silence for a moment. "I guess we ought to pray now," Sam said. "I've done some bad things, and I'd like to make sure God's not angry with me when I die."

"We don't have a lot of time, Sam," Ralph said.

Sam spoke in a low voice, careful that only Adam and Ralph could hear. "I killed Joe Lincoln. I've already said I was sorry. And I helped my brothers kill those men who murdered our father. Now I feel bad about that too. And I took part in a lynching when I was fifteen or sixteen."

Sam stopped. Adam held his breath and hoped that he had finished. He felt sick. Ralph waited, and finally asked, "Is that it, Sam?"

"No. There was another lynching. A boy named Cletus. A Klan lynching. I was eighteen. That's all I can say."

Adam remembered the other picture in Lee's book, and the date under it. The horror will never end, he thought.

"I didn't kill those Kramer boys," Sam said, his voice shaking. "I had no business being there, and I was wrong to be involved. But I didn't kill those boys. That bomb was wired by someone else, not me. I believed it was supposed to go off in the middle of the night, when no one would be anywhere near it. The other person set the bomb to go off much later. I suspect he intended to kill people."

Adam heard the words, understood them, but could not speak. Ralph said gently, "Pray with me, Sam."

The unmistakable voice of Colonel Nugent broke the calm. The door opened. He marched in, six guards behind him. "Sam, it's time to go to the Isolation Room," he said. "It's eleven o'clock."

The three men stood, side by side. The cell door opened, and Sam stepped out. He turned and put his arms around the chaplain. "Thanks," he said. Ralph Griffin pushed past the guards and left. He found a dark corner and wept like a child. He would not see Sam again.

"Let's go," Sam said. The walk to the Isolation Room took only seconds. The door on the opposite wall was shut. It led to the chamber.

"At 11.55 I will enter through that door," Nugent told them. "At that time, we'll go into the Chamber Room." He made a quick exit.

Suddenly, they were alone. One more hour.

◆

Two prison vans rolled to a stop by the ambulance. Inside were nine of the people chosen to witness the execution, most of them reporters.

Nugent was waiting for them. He hurriedly guided them through the open door into a small room where two rows of folding chairs were waiting, facing a wall of black curtains. "On the other side of these curtains," Nugent explained dramatically, "is the Chamber Room. The prisoner will be brought in at five minutes before twelve, secured in the chair, the door locked. The curtains will be opened at exactly midnight, and when you see the chamber the prisoner will already be inside it, less than two feet from the windows. Things will happen quickly after that."

The arrival of the governor's helicopter caused some excitement along the front entrance of Parchman. Another prison van was waiting. McAllister got in quickly, while cameras raced to film the van, and minutes later it stopped near to the ambulance behind MSU. Nugent met the governor and took him into the witness room, where he took a seat in the front row.

The ten of them sat in silence, staring at the black curtains and anxiously checking their watches.

♦

The end came quickly. At exactly 11.55 there was a knock on the door. As Adam jumped to his feet, Sam pointed a finger at him. "Listen to me," he said firmly. "You can walk in there with me, but you cannot stay."

"I know. I don't want to stay, Sam."

"Good." Sam reached forward and took Adam by the shoulders. Adam pulled him close.

"Tell Lee I love her," Sam said, his voice breaking. "I'm not mad at her for not coming." Adam nodded and struggled not to cry. "Give my love to the rest of the family. I'm sorry about all this, Adam. It's a terrible weight for you all to carry."

"We'll do fine, Sam."

"I know. I'll die a proud man, son, because of you."

"I'll miss you," Adam said, the tears now running down his cheeks.

Nugent went first into the Chamber Room, then Sam, then Adam. The execution team were there, but they all looked away from Sam. Adam stopped just inside the door and watched as Sam was secured into the chair. For a moment, Adam's eyes met Sam's. He was looking at his grandfather for the last time.

Nugent stood in the door of the chamber. "Any last words, Sam?" he asked.

"Not for you. It's time for Adam to leave."

Adam made his way toward the exit, and looked back. The executioner was reaching for a lever.

Suddenly, Adam wanted to get as far away from the place as he could. Outside, he leaned against the ambulance for a second, afraid that he was going to be sick. He knew that at that moment his grandfather was in the chamber struggling to breathe, his lungs burning with the poison. As he walked away, he began to cry. He cried for Sam, for the terrible way he was being forced to die. He cried for the whole Cayhall family and their miserable history.

Chapter 14   A New Dawn

The first pink light of sunrise began to shine over a hill above Clanton. It turned to yellow, then to orange. There were no clouds, just brilliant colors against the dark sky.

Shadows fell toward Adam from the rows of gravestones. He'd been there for a couple of hours. He had driven blindly away from Parchman, and eventually found himself near Clanton. He went to the graveyard, where he'd found the grave with the name of his grandmother, Anna Gates Cayhall, and rested against the stone. Four little red flags had been placed in the ground next to his grandmother's last resting place. Another grave would be dug there.

A car door closed somewhere behind him, and a figure walked toward him. Suddenly, Lee was standing beside him.

"What are you doing here?" he asked. She lowered herself and sat next to him. "Where the hell have you been, Lee?"

"In treatment."

"You could've called, at least."

"Don't be angry, Adam, please. I need a friend." She leaned a head on his shoulder. Her face was sad and hollow.

"I tried to see Sam," she said. "I drove to Parchman last night. They said it was too late."

Adam softened. "He asked about you at the end. He asked me to tell you he loved you." She started crying. "He went out with strength and courage."

"You know where I've just been?" Lee asked.

"No. Where?"

"I've been to our old home. It burned beautifully. The whole house went up in one huge fire."

"Are you serious?"

"It's true. I'm not worried – I bought the place last week. Paid thirteen thousand dollars to the bank. If you own it, then you can burn it, right?"

"How – ?"

"Gasoline. Here, smell my hands." She put them under his nose. They bore the unmistakable smell of gasoline.

"But why?"

"Evil things happened there. It was filled with ghosts and spirits. Now they're gone."

A dirty truck entered the graveyard through the iron gates, and drove slowly along the path. It stopped at a small building in a corner. Three black men slowly got out.

"I'm not going back to Chicago, Lee," said Adam.

"What?"

"I'm changing jobs."

"To do what?"

"Death penalty work. I'll be spending more time at Parchman."

She rubbed her face and pulled back her hair. "I guess you know what you're doing."

"Maybe."

The three men were standing next to an old yellow mechanical digger.

"I have an idea," said Lee. "There's a little café near here where Sam used to take me and Eddie on our birthdays. Let's see if it's open." She was excited and getting to her feet. "Come on. I'm hungry."

In the distance, an engine started. It echoed through the graveyard. Adam stopped to listen, and Lee turned to see it. The digger was moving. It started moving in low gear, very slowly past the rows of graves. Then it stopped and turned.

It was coming their way.

ACTIVITIES

Chapters 1–2

Before you read

1 Sam Cayhall is in prison, on death row. What do you think happens to people who live there? What sort of crime do you think Sam committed?

2 Find the words in *italics* in your dictionary. They are all in the story.
   a Discuss possible connections between these words:
   - *Negro* and *racism*
   - *fuse* and *dynamite*
   - *execute* and *chamber*
   - *prosecute* and *appeal*
   b Which of the four words below describes:
   - a part of a garden?
   - a person? (two words)
   - a level of government?
   terrorist   federal   patio   member

After you read

3 Work in pairs. Act out the telephone conversation between Adam and Lee in which Adam tells Lee that he will be coming to Memphis, and what he will be doing there.

4 Explain who you think is most guilty for the death of the Kramer twins, and why. To what extent do others share that guilt?

Chapters 3–5

Before you read

5 Adam drives to the prison to meet his grandfather for the first time. How do you think he is feeling? What is he going to say to Sam?

6 Find these words in your dictionary. Use them to complete the sentences below.
   briefcase   colonel   confidential   cyanide   inmate
   jumpsuit   lethal   pardon   superintendent   supreme

a A death row ..... lives in a tiny cell. He wears a red ..... when he leaves his cell.

b George Nugent was a ..... in the army. He is now assistant ..... at the prison.

c ..... is a very poisonous substance. Its effects can be ......

d Adam promises Sam that he will not talk to the media. The case will be completely ......

e He carries important documents to the prison in his ......

f The highest court is the ..... court. If it rejects your appeal, your only hope is a ..... from the state governor.

After you read

7 Who is speaking, and what are they talking about?

    a "Not a good day to see Sam."

    b "You Jew boys never give up, do you?"

    c "Frankly, I don't think I can cope with this one."

    d "I was not a very good rich woman."

    e "I have a great idea about how to save your life."

Chapters 6–8

Before you read

8 Adam goes to see the FBI agent who was in charge of the Kramer bombing case. What does he want to ask him?

9 There are four levels of court which Adam has to deal with. Put them in order of importance, the lowest first.

    a The Fifth Circuit Court of Appeals

    b The Mississippi Supreme Court

    c The United States Supreme Court

    d The federal district court

10 Are these statements true or false? Use a dictionary to check the words in *italics*.

    a If the governor agrees to *clemency*, Sam will not be executed.

    b A *lynching* is an execution carried out after a person has been tried and found guilty under the law.

    c If someone is *ineffective* at their job, they do it badly.

    d A court's *proceedings* are often very formal.

    e In a courtroom, the judges sit on the *bench*.

After you read

11 Why are these important to the story?

    a a note addressed *Dear Adam*

    b a tree in the Cayhalls' backyard

    c a photograph in an old book

12 Work in pairs. Act out the scene in which Eddie (with his toy soldier) and Lee meet in the woods after the killing of Joe Lincoln.

Chapters 9–11

Before you read

13 The title of Chapter 11 is 'Confessions.' Who do you think has confessions to make, and what are they?

14 Describe the work of these people. Use a dictionary to help you.

    a chaplain   a psychiatrist

After you read

15 Answer these questions.

    a Why has Wedge come to see Sam? Is he successful, do you think?

    b What does the chaplain think about the death penalty? Does his opinion surprise you?

    c What happens to Sam, the rabbit? What do you think about this?

    d What does Sam ask his brother Donnie to do? How does this request make Donnie feel, and why?

16 Imagine you are Sam, standing alone in the exercise yard at Parchman and watching the sun rise. Talk about the thoughts that are going through your head.

Chapters 12–14

Before you read

17 How do you think the story will end for:

    a Sam Cayhall?   **b** Adam Hall?   **c** Aunt Lee?

18 Which word has a similar meaning to *competence*?

appreciation   innocence   ability   difference

Use a dictionary to check your answer.

After you read

19 Discuss how these people feel about Sam at the end of the story. Give reasons for your opinions.

a Adam   **b** Lee   **c** Nugent   **d** McAllister

Writing

20 You are the photographer who photographed the lynching of the young black man. Write your diary entry for that day, explaining how you became involved.

21 Write Sam's letter of apology to Ruth Kramer, to be read after his death.

22 You are one of the newspaper reporters who witnessed Sam's execution. Write a report of the event.

23 You are Adam. It is a year after Sam's execution. Write a letter to Lee and tell her what you are doing now.

24 "One of Grisham's gifts is that he is able to make the reader sympathetic even to characters who are, in many ways, extremely unpleasant." How true is this of *The Chamber*?

25 Is it right that Sam is executed for his crime? Give reasons for your opinion.

Answers for the Activities in this book are published in our free resource packs for teachers, the Penguin Readers Factsheets, or available on a separate sheet. Please write to your local Pearson Education office or to: Marketing Department, Penguin Longman Publishing, 5 Bentinck Street, London W1M 5RN.